The route of my thirteen-thousand-five-hundred-mile journey through Russia

Map courtesy of *New York Herald Tribune*

# Red Plush and Black Bread

What Marguerite Higgins, the Pulitzer Prize-winning reporter of the New York *Herald Tribune,* set out to write was a first-hand, eye-opening account of life today in the forbidden Soviet countries. What she produced, in this remarkable book, is much more than that: the recent "Summit" conference at Geneva, and the events following it are the concern of the final chapters. She sounds a warning against the current "sweetness and light" policy of the Russians, and gives ominous evidence that in the red plush glove there still is clenched a fist of iron. Her skillful interpretation of these developments brings the rest of the book into sharp focus and adds immeasurably to the timeliness and importance of RED PLUSH AND BLACK BREAD.

Miss Higgins' trip behind the Iron Curtain lasted ten weeks and took her more than 13,500 miles through Siberia, Soviet Central Asia, the Caucasus, White Russia, and the Ukraine. She was the first American correspondent to get a visa to Russia after restrictions against visitors were relaxed, and was, therefore, the first roving news representative to enter Russia since the Stalin era.

Everywhere she talked to people. She asked (and got some remarkable answers to) questions about what the Russian people say and think—and eat and wear and drink and ride in, bathe in, and sleep in. This is a unique study and a fascinating one. The many photographs give an added dimension to the story—particularly when one realizes Marguerite Higgins was arrested sixteen times for taking them.

*By Marguerite Higgins*

WAR IN KOREA

NEWS IS A SINGULAR THING

RED PLUSH AND BLACK BREAD

# Red Plush and Black Bread

by Marguerite Higgins

*Illustrated with Photographs by the Author*

DOUBLEDAY & COMPANY, INC., GARDEN CITY, N. Y. 1955

*Library of Congress Catalog Card Number: 55-11332*

*To William E. Hall*

# Contents

## Introduction

This book is an eyewitness account of Russia as I saw it and Soviet policy as I have experienced it and heard it analyzed by scholars and diplomats, particularly those on the scene in Moscow.

It was a difficult book to write because I had accumulated an unusually large mass of material. Until the time of my visit much of Russia had been almost as inaccessible to Westerners as the moon. Therefore, every sight and sound, every human reaction seemed noteworthy. In two and a half months and nearly fourteen thousand miles I filled fifteen notebooks. When it came to writing this book, I wanted to select only the incidents and anecdotes that were the most revealing of attitudes and conditions inside the country.

I approached the Russian assignment with a background

of extensive research on the subject of negotiating with the Russians, which I had undertaken under a grant from the Guggenheim Foundation. I would like in this space to express once again my appreciation to the Foundation for the honor and trust of being selected for a fellowship.

I agree with those who say that there are no real experts on Russia—only people possessing varying degrees of ignorance. Because of the complexity of the subject that I have chosen to deal with, the issues are in terms of a professional observer's concrete personal experience. This book is a reporter's report.

*Geneva, Switzerland, July 26, 1955*

## Prologue

Long before I visited the Soviet Union, I had a conversation with Max Reimann, West German Communist leader, whose words persistently came into my mind as I traveled through Russia.

"If the Russians put on a real peace offensive," Reimann asked, "will it be possible for a democracy such as the United States to stay armed and to keep on voting huge subsidies for Europe and elsewhere? And if you do not, how can you possibly avoid a depression? And once there is a depression half our battle is already won."

I do not agree with Reimann's low opinion of American resourcefulness. But I think this conversation, which I recorded in an article written in midsummer of 1949, throws interesting light on present Communist motives and on a school of Communist thought which even then saw

that Stalin's tough tactics had been carried much too far—
so far that they had boomeranged. For it was Stalin's
unrelenting hostility, of course, that forced Western unity
and caused the United States and Europe to rearm.

As I have often heard America's top officials remark, if
in the early postwar years Russia had had sense enough
to play on American gullibility and to behave in a friendly
fashion she might well have had a clear path for what she
wanted. For the United States was at the time disarming
in a speedy and drastic fashion. Not only that, we were
even considering extending the Soviet Union credits,
amounting to ten billion dollars. As it was, the alarm wasn't
really sounded until the Communist take-over in Poland
and the Communist coup in Czechoslovakia.

It is true that the rapid swing of American public opinion
about Russia is one of the great problems this country
faces in trying to steer a sensible course vis-à-vis the expanded Communist empire.

The Geneva Big Four Conference is a case in point. As
one of our top American negotiators put it, "Two years ago
I was being denounced for even suggesting we should
negotiate with the Russians. Now I am made to feel like
an international spoilsport for pointing out that although
the Russians at Geneva have smiled and smiled they have
made not a single concession of substance, and that in
fact the only important concession came from President
Eisenhower." (The latter agreed that the problem of European security should precede the question of German
reunification, although the two remained linked in the
agenda referred to the foreign ministers.)

As Communist First Party Secretary Nikita S. Khruschev himself stated in a newspaper interview in early spring of 1955, Russia expects eventually that Communism will "gain the upper hand in the world." After my own travels and observations of Russia and the Russians I have no doubt that the present "collective leadership" will proceed in this attempt "to gain the upper hand" with far more intelligence, flexibility, and attention to public relations than was displayed by the late Joseph Stalin. That is why I agree with those who consider Russia today far more of a challenge to our world that Stalin's Russia ever was.

The journey that led to these conclusions began in Finland. . . .

*Red Plush and Black Bread*

## CHAPTER ONE

## *"To Whom It May Concern"*

The Russian police state has such a notorious reputation for conspiracy and blackmail that the prospect of my journey there made me rather conspiratorial myself. In the last few hours before leaving for the Finland station I sat down in my hotel room in Helsinki and wrote this letter:

*To Whom It May Concern:*

This is being written to counteract any statements made by me in the event that I should be arrested in the Soviet Union. This letter constitutes advance denial of any injurious utterances whatsoever against the United States that might be attributed to or actually delivered by me as a result of duress or torture.

*Sincerely,*

MARGUERITE HIGGINS

Then I mailed the letter to a friend of mine in the United States Department of State to be held pending my safe return west of the Iron Curtain.

Second, I went meticulously through my purse sorting and discarding all foreign money. I looked especially for stray coins or foreign paper money that would call attention to my recent trips to Indo-China and South Korea.

Third, I hunted through the crevices of my purse for calling cards, hotel receipts, or other miscellaneous documents that could reveal identities of friends or my recent whereabouts. I tore all the documents up.

Fourth, I mailed my address book home.

Finally I made arrangements so that the American Minister in Finland would start asking the Russians about my welfare if after four days he had not received a wire reporting my safe arrival.

What about possible Russian police surveillance of my activities? I had fixed my attitude on this problem as soon as I heard that my Russian visa had finally been granted (after a four-month wait). I had decided that I would make determined efforts to inform myself precisely on Russian regulations governing foreigners and observe those regulations exactly. Within the framework of the rules I'd gather all the facts I could. I'd have nothing to hide, and if the Russians wanted to go to all the trouble of having someone follow me around, that would be their business— so long as they didn't interfere with me directly.

The same evening, safely aboard the Russian International Express, I felt less apprehensive. I was escorted to the train by a Finnish-speaking official of the United States

Information Service. As we took in the scene we both commented that the bustle of leave-taking and farewell was so like that anywhere in the world one could imagine it to be just a routine departure. I presented my ticket, bought at the Helsinki branch of the Soviet Union's Intourist Bureau, to the Russian conductor, who, I noted, was wearing a black uniform and stiff cap similar to those worn in America by train officials. As the conductor confirmed that my ticket was in order he disarmed me considerably by showing that he understood my beginner's Russian (based on sixteen and a half hours at Berlitz and some intensive study of Bondar's Russian grammar). I'm afraid I caused him some consternation by asking for a glass of water. There was only one canister and *one* glass for the whole car. The conductor explained that *chai* (tea) would be served immediately and seemed to think it most eccentric that anyone would be interested in plain drinking water. Then he led me to my compartment. It turned out to be shared by three fat Danish women. They formed part of a Danish delegation that had been officially invited by the Russian Government to visit Moscow.

The International Express looked old-fashioned but cleaner than I'd expected. The sheets on my berth were worn but spotless. Of course, this was the first class or "soft car" and was specially reserved for foreigners and VIP Russians. I made a mental note to have at least one ride in the "hard cars," where the seats are made of wood and are completely cushionless. It is the cheapest accommodation and the one that serves the average Russian.

The only Russian in the international car (besides the

conductor and his assistant) was a young Russian youth
leader who said he had been visiting relatives in Finland.
Privately I doubted his story. At the time Russian authorities still restricted travel outside the country so tightly that
it was out of the question for any ordinary Russian to go
abroad on an ordinary personal mission. The only person
on the train with whom the Russian boy had any extensive
conversation was a Norwegian student of chemistry. I was
surprised to learn that the young Norwegian will spend a
year at Moscow University as an exchange student.

"The Russians are more friendly with us Europeans than
with you Americans," the Norwegian said. "And we Europeans are less prejudiced than America about the Russians."

We left the Finland station on schedule at 11 P.M.

## CHAPTER TWO

*First Impressions*

The border point on the Scandinavian route to Leningrad and the rest of Russia is the city of Viborg. It used to be a Finnish town. The Russians seized it during the "preventive war" the Soviet Union waged against the Finns back in 1939.

Despite all I'd heard about the strictness of Russian border inspections I had only one difficulty. It occurred when the uniformed customs officer, a somewhat frozen-faced but correct gentleman, insisted on taking away my copy of *Good Housekeeping* magazine, which I had brought along because I had an article in it. The customs officer, who spoke English, said he wanted to check with his superiors on whether possession of such a magazine was permissible. What bothered him, I think, were the photographs of refrigerators, shiny kitchens, and home decora-

tions. These illustrations would make it obvious to any
Russian that there are lots of things for sale in the United
States that are not available to the Russians. After we had
reboarded the train, the magazine was returned to me just
before we pulled out.

My first encounter with Soviet prices was at the Viborg
railway station restaurant, where we breakfasted. Even
though I'd been warned about prices, they were still a
shock. One hard-boiled egg and tea costs four rubles, or
one American dollar at the official rate of exchange. You
pay extra for butter, jam, and bread. A full breakfast of
fruit (grapes), ham and eggs and coffee costs more than
twenty rubles, or five dollars.

Everybody knows that the Soviet-imposed exchange rate
of four rubles to the dollar is artificial, for the dollar is
worth at least ten rubles. The State Department thinks
that the Russians maintain this artificial exchange rate so
as to make it as difficult as possible for American Embassy
personnel and other United States citizens who are visiting
the U.S.S.R. I can understand why there are only four
permanent representatives of American news-gathering
agencies stationed in Russia. Even if the Russians should
suddenly become more liberal with visas, most newspapers
couldn't afford to keep a correspondent in Moscow.

The Viborg railway station must date back a long time,
probably to the period when the Czars of Russia still ruled
all Finland. The dining room had enormously high ceilings
and the inevitable red plush curtains. I call the color "dried-
blood red" because it is so dark. To me these curtains are

depressingly heavy, both in texture and color. But to the Russians they seem to be the ultimate in luxury.

Other depressing notes that morning were the conversations I'd been having with the twelve men and women in the Danish delegation, who included teachers, doctors, and editors of small-town newspapers. Only one of the total was Communist. The rest seemed leftish and neutralist— the type who interpret the smallest token from Russia as true evidence of the Soviet Union's good intentions toward its neighbors. The Communist, a bluff, energetic, and highly talkative man, was a member of the Danish parliament. He flouted his open-collared shirt and lack of tie proudly, just like those men enamored of *la Bohème* who stick to berets instead of more orthodox hats.

From what I'd already heard in England, Sweden, and Finland and from what the Danes told me, it was clear that the Russians were pushing their new tactic of diplomacy by exchange of delegations very energetically. As part of Russia's campaign to win friends and influence people in Europe and Asia hundreds of easily controllable groups —doctors from England, engineers from Finland, students from Italy—are being officially invited these days for a red-carpet tour of Moscow.

The Danes told me that the Russians were footing the entire bill for their visit. Not only was the Soviet Government paying for the round trip from Denmark and Moscow and back but also picking up the check for food, liquor, hotel rooms, and theater tickets. Even tips. And with thoroughness that is characteristic of the Russians when they really want to do something, they have arranged hotel space, taxi service, trips through factories and mines, outings on the Volga River steamer, attendance at the Bolshoi Theater concerts and ballets. The difference between the way the Russians fete these delegations and the treatment accorded the regular press corps is striking. For instance, almost every foreign delegation tours a collective farm, but not a single Western correspondent assigned to Moscow has been granted this privilege in seven years.

Most distressing to me personally was my conversation with a Danish educator, the dean of a small pedagogical school in Copenhagen. The upshot of our exchange was the Dane's declaration that "the people of Denmark would prefer Russian rule to another war."

"But isn't this playing into Russia's hands?" I asked. "If you advertise your unwillingness to fight you encourage the Russians to make impossible demands. If Russia were to be told in advance that there would be no retaliation for the use of force against a given country, she would be tempted to move in, don't you think?"

"It can't be helped," said the Dane.

Then he asked me a question.

"I heard someone say you were a correspondent during the war in Korea. I thought everyone who ever experienced combat believed that nothing could be worse than war?"

"No," I replied. "There are things worse than war," and let it go at that.

I had been briefly tempted to quote the passage from President Eisenhower's speech to the effect that "a soldier's pack is not so heavy as a prisoner's chains." Or to describe the slow torture of a people like the Poles, who during the Communist take-over lost more human beings in arrests, mass deportations, and executions than they had suffered in four years of war against the Nazis. But I was too depressed to argue. And it hardly seemed an appropriate environment for debate about possibilities of war with the Communist world.

So instead I listened to the same Danish educator as he harangued the group of delegates gathered in my compartment about the way America had "succumbed to the demagogy of McCarthy."

"But," I finally protested, "McCarthy and his followers are a small faction in a very large country. There are many Americans who do not agree with his methods and say so. In Russia police state terror is an accepted part of life. Yet would you criticize Russia to a Russian the way you criticize America to me?"

"No," said the Dane, "probably not. But we don't expect anything of Russia."

At about sixty kilometers from Leningrad our train paused for three quarters of an hour. It turned out that we were waiting for a new engine to be switched on. Through the train window I observed a small station on the edge of what appeared to be a small town set in the lovely pine forests of this area. Seeing that the Danish delegation had clambered off the train and were strolling in the sun, I followed suit. Even though the sky was a bright shimmering blue, the temperature this August day in this northern latitude reminded me of the golden sparkle of an October morning in New York.

The first sight that caught my eye was a group of ditch-diggers working on the road parallel to the small rail station. The majority of those wielding primitive picks and shovels were women. I think I'm beginning to understand why the Russians do use women for so much hard labor. For in this group the women were more robust-looking than the men. The muscles bulged in their calves and they had plump, solid-looking bodies and big arms. Their clothes were of cotton or other coarse cloth and were of a kind definitely suitable for ditchdigging.

Because I'd heard so much about Russian hostility to foreigners and because I didn't want to create a scene, I hesitated to approach the ditchdiggers. These considerations didn't bother the Danish Communist. After informing the laborers that he was a "Communist comrade," the Dane asked how long they worked (eight hours), how many days a week (six), and what they did on vacations (stayed home and rested or went to workers' sanatoriums).

Then one of the lady ditchdiggers spoke up and said, "Do women do this kind of work in your country?"

"Well," said the Danish Communist, looking a little embarrassed, "not exactly."

At the train station in Leningrad I was met, as I'd requested in my telegram from Helsinki, by a representative of Intourist, the official bureau for handling travelers.

The Intourist representative turned out to be Irina, a handsome blond girl who was friendly in an antiseptic sort of way, as a hospital nurse might be with a patient from whom she expected difficulty. Irina was wearing a bright blue sheer wool dress. It was the first good-looking outfit I'd seen in Russia. She could afford it. The Intourist girl guides are part of Russia's elite, both in salary and special privileges. They earn about 1,200 rubles a month; at the official rate of exchange this amounts to $300. Irina told me that she had all her clothes made from patterns by a dressmaker in an *atelier* (the Russians have borrowed the word from the French). The Intourist guide added that all Russian women who have any money at all use ateliers rather than select ready-made clothes from a department store.

At the train station a porter was on hand to carry my luggage, which was limited to one suitcase and one small typewriter. He charged 5 rubles ($1.25) for each piece! I couldn't help thinking what capitalists American porters would become if they collected $2.50 for every two bags they carried. I also decided, not being a capitalist myself, that from now on I would carry my own luggage.

The waiting Intourist car was a four-door Pobeda (meaning Victory). I'd seen Pobeda models in Finland, to which Russians are exporting these vehicles despite the continuing shortage of automobiles in the U.S.S.R. A Pobeda, Irina told me, costs 16,000 rubles, or at the legal rate of exchange, some $4,000. But even if one has the money there is a ten-month wait. The style of the Russian Pobeda is about equal to that of an American Ford or Chevrolet of 1936-40 vintage. The Russian gearshift is the regular old-fashioned style. There are no gadgets. But the car looks sturdy and is comfortable. Irina claimed that it could go 100,000 kilometers over Russia's bumpy roads without undergoing repairs.

As we approached my hotel, the Astoria, I asked the question I'd been waiting a long time to put to a real live Soviet citizen in his own country: "Irina, would you say that there have been any visible improvements in Russian life since the death of Stalin [March 1953]?"

"Well," answered Irina cagily, "there have been improvements, but I don't see any connection with the death of Stalin. It's perfectly logical that improvements should be especially noticeable at this time. After all, right after the war the main effort was in reconstruction [more important —though Irina didn't say it—in rearmament]. Now with most of the reconstruction done the government can turn more to the specific needs of the people."

"Could you give me some example of improvements?" I asked.

"As you know [I didn't], food is no longer rationed," Irina answered, "and in the general price cuts last April [1954] there were important reductions in the cost of butter, bread, meat, and other staples. Also there are more varieties of food available. Clothing costs much less than it used to. And now it's possible to buy such things as television sets, whereas a few years ago you could only buy a set if you were very, very important. Demand is still bigger than the supply and you have to wait a long time. But at least the television sets are actually on sale in the stores."

And then Irina focused her big baby-blue eyes on me and asked, "Do you have television in America?"

The Astoria looked to me like those massive old-fashioned hotels that were built on lower Park Avenue, New York, in the early part of this century. I was received at the hotel by the director of Intourist, a good-looking woman in her early forties wearing a mannish suit of nondescript brown material. She confirmed receipt of my telegram, which had requested Intourist Bureau to arrange interviews with the Mayor of Leningrad and various prominent political and professional Russians in the city.

"It will be impossible," the Intourist director said. "You cannot stay in Leningrad at all. Your passport says your destination is Moscow. You must take the next train. It leaves in two hours."

"I'm afraid *that* will be impossible," I said, finding myself astonished at the boldness with which I was opposing the will of a representative of the Soviet police state.

"Now look here," I continued, "I went over my itinerary carefully with the Russian Embassy in Washington. It was understood that I would stay at least three days in Leningrad."

Finally after much haggling and mysterious telephoning it was agreed that I could, after all, stay in Leningrad. About the interviews, she "would see."

With this skirmish won, I turned and headed for the elevator and my hotel room. I was startled to be intercepted by a male voice saying, "Hey, are you an American?"

"Yes," I said, turning around.

There stood a pleasant-faced man of medium height. He was wearing a suit that I could recognize as being of high quality.

"Well, I'm an American too," he said. "Say, it's really amazing to bump into an American woman in this part of the world."

My first reaction, I must confess, was of being cheated. Here I was feeling very much the lone explorer on a strange and dangerous continent. Then within my first twelve hours in Russia I walk into my hotel and the first person I run into is another American. But I was soon very grateful for the encounter. For this American businessman had a vast store of knowledge about getting along in Russia.

He was a fur buyer. And although this was to be just a short trip he had lived in Russia for four straight years during the war. His first piece of advice was to buy Intourist coupons. For nineteen dollars a day this tourist rate provides three meals a day and tea, the payment of the hotel room, and two hours of car hire. I took his advice with thanks. I was doubly thankful that evening after looking at the prices on the menu. Without coupons dinner would have come to twenty dollars. Add to that the cost of the hotel room, twenty dollars, and cost of other meals, plus car hire, I could easily have found myself paying a hundred dollars a day just to subsist.

My hotel room proved to be comfortable if rather ugly. An equal in ugliness to the red plush curtains that draped the windows was a desk lamp shrouded in orange silk dangling a heavy fringe. This violent clash in colors which

I was to find everywhere in European Russia was supple-
mented by the red and purple flowers in the printed rug.
The bathroom was adequate, having an old-fashioned but
delightfully big bathtub, flush toilet, and toilet paper.

The next step after unpacking was to find out how to
send a telegram so that I could notify the American Minister in Helsinki that all was well. The post office, Intourist
explained, was three blocks away from the hotel. My trip
there was my first venture out on my own and I felt as
excited as if I were about to climb Mount Everest. I think
I half expected that at any moment a big hand would clap
me on the shoulder and a voice would say, "Off to the salt
mines with you!"

All that happened was that I got lost, arriving at the
local post office instead of the international post office.
Hearing my queries, an English-speaking Russian girl
kindly took me under her wing, guided me to the correct
address, and helped me explain my needs to the clerk. As
we were walking back in the direction of the hotel I said,
"If you should ever come to America I hope you will meet
with equal courtesy."

"America!" she fairly shouted. "Is that where you come
from? I thought you were English!"

And she abruptly turned on her heel and walked away.

I think she was genuinely scared. I could understand it—
looking at it from her point of view. Even with my imperfect Russian I could glean enough from the papers to see
that they were carrying on a virulent hate-America campaign. Comparatively speaking, the press is buttering up
the English. So helping the Englishwoman would coincide

with government policy but helping an American might be dangerous.

Back at the hotel I could not shift my mind from the incident. "I hope it's not an omen," I thought.

Although most of the buildings in Leningrad badly need paint and sprucing up, the architecture of this city is attractive. Obviously many of the architects took Paris as a model. One notices the resemblance particularly along the embankments of the rivers and canals that intersect the city.

On the fourth day of my visit and just prior to my departure for Moscow I took a long walk about the city trying to sort out first impressions. In looking back over the lengthy entry in my diary I find that most of these impressions were borne out by the rest of what I saw in Russia though at that early date I did not yet grasp the meaning of the pattern.

My diary states: "What has been most striking in Leningrad are the contrasts that one sees everywhere. I was astonished to see that Leningrad's main street is dominated by the rush of bright and shiny new buses painted red and white and remarkably similar in style to Madison Avenue buses in New York. Yet on the same street on which these buses operate one can see kerchiefed women in faded patched cottons sweeping the streets with primitive brooms made of twigs.

"There is a brand-new park of culture and rest where the phlox grows fantastically tall and is as beautiful as any I've ever seen. This park also boasts a giant sports stadium with elaborate gymnastic equipment, including special rooms for boxing, wrestling, and tumbling. Yet there remain areas in this city where streets are unpaved and turn to mud when it rains.

"A new department store has been opened and it is thronged. Yet the shoppers are dressed shabbily. There are kerchiefed peasant women in run-down shoes and materials of lesser quality than America's cheapest basement offerings. The men generally have on shiny suits with frayed shirts and open collars. It seems incredible that they can be more than window-shoppers.

" 'You don't understand,' Irina keeps telling me. 'People still have more money than there are things to buy. They have been forced to save because for years there was nothing to spend it on. There were no dresses or shoes available to the majority. Even though things are better, prices due to the shortages are high. And a worker's wife isn't going to wear her good dress out shopping. That's why so many look a little shabby.'

"Tattered and peeled as they are, the façades of the apartment buildings on Leningrad's embankments still have a kind of aristocratic grandeur. Inside the building it's a different picture, as one can see by peering in from the street.

"The impression is of terrific overcrowding. As many as four or five couches or beds in one room, laundry hanging up all over the place, as in slum dwellings, utensils such as pots and pans, cups and saucers piled on tables, chairs, beds, and even the floor. It is clear that an enormous number of Leningrad families make one room do as bedroom, living room, and dining room for the entire family.

"The most exasperating facet of the journey so far has been the dealings with Intourist. The director of the bureau said it would be impossible to arrange any of the interviews because *every individual I requested to see* was involved in special conferences. Despite all her assurances I don't believe she even asked for the interviews. As one of her subordinates put it, 'It is very difficult unless it has been cleared in advance by Moscow.' "

So far the only Russians with whom I'd had any real dealing were the Intourist interpreters and they certainly were frightened of doing anything on their own or anything slightly unusual. It took a long argument before I could persuade my Intourist interpreter to ride with me on the electric train to the seashore village where she and her mother had rented a few rooms for the summer in a *dacha* (individual home).

"But why don't you ride in an Intourist car? It is better than the train," Irina said.

"Because I want to find out what it's like to ride on an electric train in Russia and who the passengers are. I can't see this from an automobile," I replied.

I added that I was curious to see what a place in the country consisted of and visit the village in which a person like Irina chose to spend the summer.

We got to the *dacha* all right but Irina didn't invite me in.

"It would startle people to see a foreigner," she said.

But I think it was more than that. It was part of the inferiority complex that explained so much of the boasting that I had already encountered in virtually every Russian with whom I'd had dealings. Irina had boasted about her television set and her record collection. But I think she was afraid to let the reality compare with the boast.

From the outside the *dacha* seemed a rather substantial two-story wood house having probably five or six rooms. It badly needed paint but the garden was a magnificent testimonial to Russian black earth. The dahlias grew thick and tall, with a luxuriance enviable to any gardener.

Irina did take me to the seashore, a twenty-minute walk from the *dacha*. As we walked across the sand dunes toward the gray, cold-looking water she confided that she went swimming every day, rain or shine, before going to work.

"The sea is my friend," she said.

And for the first time I felt a sense of warmth toward her, an intuition of deep loneliness, a stirring of compassion.

Also for the first time there on the sea's edge she began to talk a little of herself. Her husband, she said, had been a naval officer killed early in the war.

"We were going to wait until after the war to have children," she added. "Now I wish we had gone ahead. At my age [thirty-eight] a woman without a child feels a sense of emptiness. If you remain without children you will feel it too."

"But won't you remarry?"

"Ah," she said. "It is not so easy. As one gets older one becomes more complicated. One is not so easily pleased. Perhaps it is best I remain with my mother."

"You get along well with your mother?"

"Get along well! I adore my mother."

On the way back to the train station Irina pointed out a number of *dachas* in the process of construction. She said it was now possible for an increasing number of Russians to own their own homes. According to a decree issued in April 1954, the Soviet Government will extend assistance to those wishing to build their own homes, including credit from the state bank. A one-room *dacha* with a kitchen and bath costs 9,000 rubles to build ($2,250). A two-room *dacha* costs 14,000 rubles ($3,500). On the return to Leningrad the electric train was very crowded, it being the rush hour. Aside from the lady conductors, what interested me the most was that there are special cars set aside for mothers and children.

And, in fact, from a psychological point of view the most interesting thing has been the behavior of the Russian children. The naturalness and liveliness is startling because it contrasts so strongly with the oddity (in Western eyes) and unnaturalness of the Russian adult. Such overdeveloped Russian traits as suspicion, fear of showing emotion, deviousness are all artificially and abnormally developed as the result of living under police state conditions. If you live in an atmosphere where a slip of the tongue can send you to a concentration camp you learn out of self-preservation to be extremely careful of what you say. The frozen-faced deadpan manner so many Russians adopt with foreigners is obviously the result of fear. But such fears haven't penetrated the consciousness of the younger children. Even with a foreigner they are friendly and gay. In Russia, just as anywhere else in the world, a three-year-old is not likely to consider your acceptability on ideological grounds but, instead, on grounds of whether you are generous with a bag of candy.

## CHAPTER THREE

## Moscow

What surprised me most in my first few days were the number of television antennae in the Soviet capital and Russian secretiveness. The latter was a quality about which I'd been warned. But the reality surpassed the warning.

The Russians are so secretive that it is impossible to locate a friend in a hotel unless you know the room number in advance. There is no such thing as just asking for him at the desk. On my first day I wanted to get in touch with a number of correspondents, including the representative of Agence France Presse, who, I had been told, resided at my hotel, the Metropole, located on Sverdlovsk Square just catercorner from the famous Bolshoi Theater. But when I asked the Russian woman administrator (equivalent of information clerk) on what floor the Western correspondent lived she told me blandly that she had no idea.

"But can't you check your roster?" I asked, explaining that I'd just arrived in Moscow, was alone, and wanted very much to reach some of my colleagues.

"No," she said, poker-faced, "our roster does not have such information."

Although it was Sunday, I finally took a taxi (seven dollars round trip) to the American embassy. The marine guard had the information I wanted. He also presented me with a list that was to prove invaluable. It contained not only the telephone numbers of the major embassies but also the numbers of prominent foreigners and various Russan Government installations of special import to a stranger: the airport, railway stations, fire department, press section. This list was a vital necessity to all Americans in Russia because the metropolitan city of Moscow had no generally available phone book! You can only telephone someone in secrecy-minded Russia if he has given you his number or you have obtained it from a mutual friend.

And I discovered that under the State Secrets Act, passed in Stalin's last days, it was in fact possible for the authorities to imprison a Soviet citizen for merely giving out a phone number to a foreigner. After Stalin's death the act was repealed.

Most Westerners shared my surprise at the television situation in Moscow. I've since concluded that the attitude with which most of us Westerners approach things Russian ends up working to the psychological advantage of the Russians.

As a very hardheaded Finnish Social Democrat put it during a visit to Moscow, "Most foreigners come to Russia expecting life to be impossible or next door to impossible. Then they find that materially, at least, things are possible or at least more so than currently pictured in the West. And so inversely Russia gets credit merely for not being as bad as the visitor had thought. In visiting Great Britain or Belgium the stranger does not immediately rush to see the auto works or the TV factory. We take for granted that these countries are capable of manufacturing autos and TV sets. But in Russia, which produces more than 40 million tons of steel a year, we are astonished that the Russians have manufactured a million TV sets since the second world war. What ought to be astonishing is that a nation of this steel capacity has turned out so few TV sets!"

(In a record-breaking month in 1954 the United States turned out more than a million TV sets in a thirty-day period.)

Television in Russia is confined to the largest cities, including Leningrad, Kiev, and Moscow. Broadcasts originating from 'these cities have a radius of only sixty-two miles. But Moscow's television director has predicted that Leningrad and Moscow would be linked by television cable in 1955. This is the target year for color television too.

One of the strangest sights in Russia today is to see two television antennae protruding from the roofs of ancient log houses in Moscow's outskirts. Although the houses are so dilapidated they literally sag sideways into the mud, each of the two families crammed into the tiny space possesses a set of its own.

Where do they get the money? To this day there is much

more money than there are things to buy in Russia. On a much vaster scale the situation in Russia resembles that of England and America in wartime, when despite a regulated economy there was shortage of goods—compared with the demand created by booming employment. In wartime America there were not enough cars, sugar was scarce, and aluminum pots and pans disappeared from the stores. In Russia it still is wartime in the sense that the vast majority of the national income still goes into armaments and heavy industry.

In America a family spends a large proportion of its money on rent and things for the home. But in Russia housing is so scarce that apartments and other living space are assigned by housing boards and allotted by square foot, with about ten feet by thirteen per person. Rents are fixed and extremely low, and even if a Russian had the money he couldn't spend it on rent because there are no expensive homes or apartments available. None have been built by the government, which of course controls all the housing, and those that are left over from Czarist times are requisitioned by the top Communist party brass. Low rents and shortages are a kind of enforced saving plan for Russia.

One can see that there are more people with money than there are luxuries to buy by visiting Gum, the new department store on Red Square. The lines of would-be purchasers before the TV sales section start forming early. In Moscow a television set with a small screen can be obtained for 1,600 rubles ($400 at the official rate of exchange). But after the order has been accepted there is a ten-month wait for delivery. The largest screen I saw was seventeen inches and models of this type range as high in price as $1,000.

In the Russian capital the two state-owned television channels operate from 7 P. M. until midnight. On one of my first nights at the Metropole the management had installed a television set in the lobby to show it off to a visiting delegation from China. The reception seemed satisfactory.

The early-evening programs are dedicated to children. They consist mainly of animated cartoons, puppet shows, and fairy tales. The variety for adults is still very limited. By far the most popular programs are live broadcasts of such events as soccer, boxing, and wrestling. The television event of the year, for instance, was the recent soccer match between the Russian Dynamo team and the British Arsenal team—a match in which the British were soundly trounced. Programs also include ballet, concerts, light variety shows, and movies made in Russia, China, and the other satellites or in such neutral countries as India.

A gastronomic surprise was the quality of the Russian ice cream, which is sold from portable stands and pushcarts that dot the sidewalks of Moscow's main thoroughfares. The ice cream is, however, extremely expensive, ranging from fifty cents to a dollar for the equivalent of an American cone. Nevertheless, after my return from Russia I couldn't resist engaging in some gentle teasing of American ice cream manufacturers. In answer to their queries I always expressed the opinion that the reason that Russia produced such good ice cream is because that country is so backward:

the Russians haven't invented artificial sugar, artificial flavoring, artificial cream, etc.

The best food in Moscow is available at the restaurants recently built under a government policy. The policy requires that every nationality in the sixteen Russian republics (Georgia, Armenia, Turkestan, etc.) should be represented by its own restaurant in Moscow. On my first night in town I was taken to the Uzbek restaurant (Soviet Central Asia) and enjoyed shashlik (skewers of lamb, onion, pickles, tomatoes broiled over an open flame), dry red wine made in Georgia (Caucasus Mountains). I also enjoyed staring at the other customers, mostly Uzbeks visiting Moscow as tourists. To me the Uzbeks appeared a cross between Mongols and Persians. I was fascinated by the geometric skull caps worn by the men and the elaborate embroidery on the jackets of both the men and women.

The newest thing in Moscow is the Leningradskaya Hotel, an architectural monstrosity but the only place in Russia where real *steak bleu* (very rare) is to be found. In the winter of 1954 the Leningradskaya waiters were ordered into black tie. It was the first appearance of formal dress since the Bolsheviks came to power.

Essential foods—bread, cereals, fats—are plentiful. It is quality and variety that are lacking. There is certainly plenty of food on the shelves and in the stores. Although the people are shabbily dressed and miserably housed, there is no doubt that the majority are healthy. They may not be eating well but they are eating enough. My very lasting respect for black bread began in those first days in Russia. This coarse bread, the taste of which I happen to like, is not only jammed with vitamins but is a natural internal regulator. And it put five pounds on me in as many days. I can understand now how it is possible for people to survive in the concentration camps on nothing but black bread.

There is, of course, no comparison whatsoever between the American standard of living and that in Russia. The shabbiness and down-at-the-heel air of most of the shoppers at Gum Department Store would provoke stares in any middle-class section of the United States.

But I think we Westerners forget that the Russians have almost no basis for comparison with the outside world and especially with America. In conversations with me the Russians confined their remarks to comparing things this year in Russia to last. There is unanimity among average Russians that conditions are somewhat better. The people seem, by their own standards, to feel a sense of material progress. (And under Mashal Bulganin's regime the planned production of consumer goods, while not as high as originally announced, was expected to be maintained at a higher rate than ever before.)

In touring Moscow's streets two things impressed me. The width of the main boulevards (it has been accomplished by wholesale demolition of buildings or by physically pushing them back) and the amount of traffic, which, however, does seem to include a lot of empty trucks.

Moscow is at its best when seen at night from the air. The bright electrically lit red stars that crown the tall buildings as well as the towers of the Kremlin give a strange ruby tracery to the pattern of lights. Otherwise, Moscow is heavy and stolid in its architecture, much of it being almost Germanic in mood.

The most beautiful buildings in Moscow are the Orthodox churches. In fact, despite its formidable high walls, the Kremlin was more beautiful than I'd expected because of the golden cupolas of the churches and the golden outline of the ancient palaces that form the skyline beyond these walls. Moscow's few skyscrapers, like the Soviet Ministry of Foreign Affairs and the brand-new thirty-two-story university built atop Leningrad Hills, have a gingerbread-icing décor displeasing to most Western tastes.

Of the Russian people my outstanding impression is robustness and vitality. Even in many of the city folk the peasant strain shows through, and indeed most are not long away from the land. These are a people who have not lost the capacity for primitive struggle for survival. It has been a hard thirty-five years for the Russian people. It has made them tough—those who survived.

In my first letter from Moscow I wrote: "All over the walls of Russian towns—Leningrad, Moscow, even small villages through which our train passed en route from Helsinki—are scrawled Foreign Minister Molotov's famous words, 'In the second half the twentieth century all roads lead to Communism.' Everywhere I've been I've encountered official propaganda of hate for the United States and distortion of what it stands for. It pounds at you interminably via the press, in the radio, in official speeches.

And as I continue observing this country, the conviction grows that, enslaved though they be, the Russians are a people whose vitality and drive it would be fatal to underestimate."

I was not surprised that this letter was not passed by the censor.

## CHAPTER FOUR

## *Some Strange Events*

It was not until I began talking with other Western newsmen in Moscow that I realized fully my journalistic good fortune in being granted a visa in the phase of Soviet policy that obtained during my trip.

First, I was the only representative of a major daily newspaper to have obtained a temporary visa since the Stalin era. And by accident of fortune I had arrived in the country at a time when the Russian Government was reopening sections of the country, including parts of Siberia, to foreign travel, whereas in postwar years foreigners had been restricted to areas within a twenty-five-mile radius of Moscow. Further, Stalin's absolute ban against photographs of any kind was being relaxed to a small degree, even though in actual practice people carrying cameras frequently were arrested by Soviet policemen. Either by

design or ignorance some policemen acted as though they
had not heard of the new regulations. Still, although much
film was being confiscated, more than ever before was
being sent out and that was better than nothing.

Finally I would have all of Russia as an exclusive story
if my requests for trips to Siberia, Soviet Central Asia, and
the Caucasus were authorized. It would be an exclusive
by default because the four permanent American correspondents in Moscow were at the time prisoners of the
spot news story; they had to keep a twenty-four-hour watch
for news breaks emanating from the official Communist
party press in Russia's capital.

In my first few weeks in Russia I constantly encountered
the question of why the Russians had chosen this time to
let me into their country. It was a question I also kept
asking myself. And indeed it seemed odd that the authorities should suddenly give a visa to a journalist whom the
Communist press had described as a "hyena of the press."
There was one very interesting theory put forward by some
veteran diplomats in Moscow. Perhaps, they said, the
Russians wanted to dramatize the so-called mellowed "new
look" by opening up the doors a crack to an individual
whom they considered a representative of the ultracapitalist
press, which, in Russian eyes, the *Herald Tribune* personi-
fied. This would give them more of a talking point than
a visa to a Communist correspondent, for instance. Even
Stalin himself had practiced this trick. He gave his interviews mainly to such persons as Kingsbury Smith of the
Hearst syndicate or visitors like Harold Stassen and Wen-
dell Wilkie. Was it possible that I had been selected for the

red-carpet treatment? Would I be able to interview the top brass, like Nikita Khrushchev, the Communist party Secretary and rumored boss of Russia?

There seemed a good case for believing that I would. For a while my journalistic hopes were high. Then I started trying to get in touch with the Soviet Foreign Office press section. No journalist can accomplish anything in Russia in the way of interviews, visits to factories or schools unless it is facilitated by the press department. But it was not until my third day in Moscow that I was even able to talk with the Soviet press chief, Mr. Katsov, and his assistant, Mr. Simonov. Finally I was in their office, sitting with them around a conference table covered with billiard-table green felt. I handed them a list of six government officials and army officers I wanted to interview, including Khrushchev and Marshal Zhukov, and the institutions I hoped to visit in Moscow. I had been warned that the only way to get anything done at all was to ask for the maximum and request that it be done in the shortest possible time. So I added that I wanted to start my trip to Soviet Central Asia and Siberia in ten days and would appreciate if the interviews could be arranged within that time.

The reaction was noncommittal. Much too noncommittal. "We'll see," they said. I began to feel the red carpet being eased right out from under me. Alarmed, I tried at least to get a definite commitment on my projected travels through the Soviet Union.

Then Mr. Katsov said, "But we have nothing to do with that. You must go through Intourist."

"But I'm not a tourist, I'm a correspondent."

"You're not a permanent correspondent. So for these travels you must apply through Intourist. Of course, if there are problems you can always tell Intourist to contact us."

I could not budge them. I began seriously to consider cutting my trip to a couple of weeks and heading for home. Then some strange events occurred that seemed to indicate that I was to be given, if not the red carpet, at least a somewhat more favorable treatment than the regular press corps, a conscientious, hard-working group of journalists up against the worst handicaps I'd ever witnessed.

The first encouraging fact was a visit to my Moscow hotel from a Russian professor of physics whom I'd met on the train trip between Leningrad and Moscow. This was a rare phenomenon because it was unheard of in Moscow for a Russian to visit any foreigner, especially if it involved visiting a hotel like the Metropole, run by agents of the secret police. The gulf maintained between foreigners and Russians had been emphasized to me by one of the veterans of Moscow, Harrison Salisbury of the New York *Times,* who was just preparing to leave for home. He told me that in his six years in Russia suspicion of foreigners had been such that he had been unable to make a single Russian friend. And, in fact, not a single Westerner I met in Moscow had ever been invited inside a Russian home.

It had to be assumed, of course, that the professor's visit had been cleared with the Moscow secret police. It would have been courting the concentration camps otherwise for him to pay a call on an American on his own initiative. But it did seem to be a sign that I was to be permitted more extensive contacts with the Russian people than any of my colleagues. Certainly more than were American diplomats, who lived isolated existences as far removed from life in Russia as are lepers from the life of the world. Such isolation is, of course, deadly to anyone seeking information. Almost any human contact with Russians, limited as it may be, can be revealing, and this is undoubtedly why the Soviet authorities made such a studied attempt for so long to separate their people and the rest of the world.

On the train the professor's conversation had been revealing for he had been voluble. And the main thing he revealed to me is that whatever success the Bolsheviks may have had in making over human nature they have certainly not succeeded in eradicating the element of human vanity. This became obvious only a few moments after the professor and I had settled down in the train compartment we had been assigned to share. (In Russia it is commonplace for men and women to share the same train compartments.) After we had introduced ourselves, the Soviet scientist began the serious conversation with this question: "I am fifty-four years old—do you think that is terribly old?"

"Of course not. In America we consider that fifty-four is right in the prime of life."

Apparently cheered, the professor pulled out some vodka, offering me some. I countered by offering him some scotch whisky out of my last bottle.

Looking as if it took great courage, he poured the scotch into a water glass and gulped nearly half a tumbler in true Russian bottoms-up style. Then he probed in his valise and got out some black bread and dried salted fish.

"We Russians think that with alcohol food is necessary for the equilibrium," he said. "But to get back to this question of age . . . I really don't mind too much being fifty, although it is kind of the end of an era and I have always been attractive to women. But this gets you into trouble too. I have been divorced once. Two children by my first wife and two children by my second wife. My present wife is very young. A schoolteacher. Very pretty and intelligent. We lead a good life. Russia values her scientists, you know. I have bought a television set and I have my own car. We have a phonograph and when friends come over we dance. In winter we go skiing. In summer we go boating. We belong to a boating club. I like sports. I watch wrestling and boxing on television. And I personally attend all the big soccer matches in the stadium . . . I can afford all this because Russia pays her scientists very well. We Russian scientists are much better treated than are the scientists in America——"

"How would you know how American scientists are treated?" I had interrupted.

"I've read about it."

"But do you honestly believe all those things printed in *Pravda?*" *Pravda* is the largest Russian newspaper.

"Well," the professor had answered rather defensively, "isn't what's printed true?"

"No, a lot of it isn't true."

But in Moscow when the professor turned up at my hotel room at the Metropole—apparently somewhat embarrassed by the big bouquet of dahlias in his hands—he was unfortunately not talkative at all. For in my room was another Russian, a young girl named Nadia, whose name and phone number had been given to me by the American furrier. She had worked as the furrier's secretary during those war years, when Russian-American friendship was the order of the day. And when I had telephoned and asked her over she had turned up. That, too, had seemed encouraging.

Afterward I couldn't help musing that this had been a strange coincidence. First I'd been told by those who should know that Russians do not dare risk normal acquaintanceship with a foreigner. Then suddenly not one but two Russians descend on me at a time. Could it have been planned that way? The certain result was that all possibility of useful conversation had been nullified. For in Nadia's presence the professor would do nothing but talk in set phrases about the glories of the Soviet Union. Nadia followed suit, and they both gave me the impression that the purpose of their visit was to impress each other with their loyalty to Bolshevism. I might as well have been reading *Pravda*.

Two days after this incident a call finally came through from the Foreign Office press section. No, there was nothing final on my trip to Siberia. No, there was no reaction on my request to see Khrushchev and company. But the press section was not completely empty-handed. I could visit a maternity home, meet the director of the Bolshoi Theater, talk with Anatoly Surov, the Stalin prize winner for poetry. Most newsworthy of all, I could be the first Western newsman to interview Galina Ulanova, the ballerina. And I'd be able to visit the famous Russian dancer in her own home.

So I decided that the visit of the professor and Nadia had been a good omen after all.

## CHAPTER FIVE

## Prima Ballerina

Galina Ulanova, whom *Time* magazine has described as the world's greatest dancer, is undisputed queen of Russia's cultural world. Statues of Ulanova adorn the Bolshoi Theater; portraits of her hang in hundreds of public buildings; poems and songs are written about her. On the days of her performances the queues before the box office lengthen dramatically and ardent balletomanes waylay theatergoers in attempts to talk them out of their tickets (I, for instance, turned down an offer of 200 rubles, or $50, for one.)

When word got around the Metropole Hotel that I had talked to Ulanova, I became a celebrity overnight. Even the sullen chambermaid warmed up. She flooded me with questions. "Is she pretty from close up? Did she answer all your questions? Is it true that in a few more years she will retire?"

The curiosity of the diplomatic set in Moscow was no less than that of the chambermaids. It did not escape my amused attention that invitations to lunches and dinners increased fourfold after the visit.

The interview was at five o'clock Sunday, on a sunny September afternoon. Ulanova lives on the eighth story of a staid brownstone block of flats having a view of the Moscow River. She herself met me at the door. Her maid had gone south for her annual vacation.

Ulanova is a lovely-looking woman; her outstanding facial features are bright blue eyes, the color of which were heightened by the olive tone of her suntanned skin. Her hair was her least attractive point. It was in a long bob and had been frizzed as if she had had a very kinky permanent wave which she hadn't bothered to have set. Her body had the litheness of that of a young girl. Her legs would have brought whistles anywhere in the world. Her gray wool dress was simple and well fitted and her black pumps lighter than the shoes worn by most Russian women.

We sat down at a round oak table in the small living room, perhaps ten feet wide by thirteen feet long, which also served as a dining room. Over the table hung a big lamp with huge white cloth shade, around which we peered as we talked. Also in the room were several cabinets made of the same heavy dark wood, a number of straight-backed chairs, and a small sofa. It could have been an apartment in an old-fashioned lower-middle-class building on New York's West Side.

Ulanova was a forthright person. She talked easily and without hesitation.

"Has your career as a ballerina brought you happiness?" I asked at one point.

"It is a strange thing," Ulanova answered. "Often after a big performance there is much applause. The audience is very pleased. I receive many curtain calls and many flowers. And yet sometimes when I return to my apartment I find there is a desert in my heart."

A desert in the heart! This was the frankest remark made to me in Russia by any Russian of importance. To realize how extraordinary is such an admission it must be understood that in Russia the government decrees that Russians shall be happy, or say they are happy. For to admit unhappiness—a desert in the heart—of any kind is to admit the workers' paradise has fallen short in giving its people the happiness about which it boasts. It may seem odd that the rulers of a country whose melancholy soul has been a distinguishing mark of character should cling adamantly to strength-through-joy themes. But they do. None denies that many facets of life in Russia involve struggle, but the Russian is supposed to enjoy the struggle. Always.

There were other highlights of the conversation with Ulanova.

"How strict are your disciplines in the Russian ballet? Can you, for instance, occasionally have a drink of vodka?"

"Of course I drink vodka," Ulanova answered. "Vodka gives you strength—and sometimes courage."

"What is your greatest wish?"

"To keep my health and strength," Ulanova said.

"Do you have any plans for retirement?" (Ulanova is in her middle forties.)

"No, I shall dance so long as I can dance well," she said.

"To what do you attribute your success?"

"Terribly hard work." This Ulanova said with the defiant emphasis of a celebrity who wants to quash notions that there is a sure and easy formula for success.

"Today is Sunday," she added, "and already I have practiced three hours. The reason I couldn't receive you before is that we have been working very long days for the filming of the ballet *Romeo and Juliet*."

Later at the Bolshoi Theater, large, plush, and glittery, I saw Ulanova dance the last act of *Romeo and Juliet*. I was disappointed, not in Ulanova's dancing but in the fact that there was so little of it in the ballet. For a large part of *Romeo and Juliet* is pageantry—the long procession carrying Juliet's body down elaborate switchback stairs takes more than ten minutes for its danceless descent—and pantomime. Moreover, although the Bolshoi obviously lavished enormous sums on the costumes and sets, the Russians, despite such huge expenditures, fail in matters of taste. Many color combinations were jarring: orange-clad ballerinas next to male dancers in harsh magenta-toned purple. But there was certainly no denying the endurance and technical skill of the Russian dancers when they got a chance to dance. I preferred such ballets as *Cinderella*, where pantomime is at a minimum and the dancers, par-

ticularly the prima ballerina, can dazzle with their pyro-
technics.

Whatever I might think of Russian ballet, Ulanova clearly did not have much regard for Western ballet and some
of its prima ballerinas. Or perhaps this was just her expression of the apparent national need to boast that everything
in the Soviet Union is bigger and better than anywhere else
in the world. In any event, when I asked about Alicia
Markova, whom Ulanova had seen do the second act in
*Swan Lake* during the International Arts Festival in Venice,
Ulanova paused only a moment.

"Markova's dancing is old-fashioned," she said. "It is
too stylized. Your ballet in the West is not as advanced as
ours. We have more lyric quality."

Lyric quality, I gathered, meant, among other things,
that the ballerina devoted great care to acting out the
character being portrayed, making her seem as close to real
life as possible, and using her own gestures and expressions
in pantomiming the role. But Ulanova did have a good
word for some of the younger ballerinas whom she had
seen dancing in Markova's company and whom she said
showed "promise."

Of her personal life Ulanova said that her husband had
died three years previously and that she had no children.

"It had to be a choice between children or career," she
said. "I have put my career above everything. I do not
regret the choice. Perhaps someday I will."

Ulanova's favorite recreations, she said, were swimming
and boating in a kayak. She liked occasionally to cook

although her cook-housekeeper generally looked after her wants. The ballerina produced an apple cake dusted with sugar which she had baked herself. She eagerly consumed a large piece of it, assuring me that she never dieted. She also served cheese, apples, bread, tea, and vodka.

Ulanova's start in ballet was a matter of chance. It began when her mother, a ballerina in Leningrad, decided to earn some extra money by teaching and included Ulanova to fill out her first class. Ulanova's talents emerged gradually. By the time she was in her twenties critics were saying that she belonged in the category of the greats.

This Russian woman is clearly not a person who takes life easily. Even today, she said, she finds herself apprehensive before important performances. And the creation of her role in the new ballets introduced by Russian choreographers is a real ordeal. She said Stravinsky had been the most difficult to combine with danceable and dramatically interesting ballets.

As a prima ballerina at the Bolshoi Theater, Ulanova is at the top of Russia's intellectual and financial elite, which includes artists, writers, famous scientists, professors, sports stars, plant managers, and Communist party bosses. Ulanova stands in the highest pay bracket. Because she performs in movies as well as on the stage, Ulanova, in a good year, could easily earn more than 100,000 rubles ($25,000), whereas the average Soviet worker earns somewhat less than 9,000 ($2,500).

By American standards Ulanova lived simply. By Russian standards she was extraordinarily well off. For in recognition of her importance and prestige the housing board had allotted her three rooms, a full kitchen, and bath all to herself.

When I said I'd like to see the rest of Ulanova's apartment, she said she'd be willing to show me around. Certainly the most beautiful object in the apartment was a painting on silk—a portrait of Ulanova in the *Swan Lake* costume. It was presented to the ballerina during the Soviet ballet troupe's tour of the Far East.

I estimated that all the rooms were about ten feet by thirteen feet or less. The bedroom adjoined the living room. It held a wardrobe, a small single bed, and several small cabinets. The third room was a kind of second sitting room. Its most notable feature was a grand piano, and Ulanova said this was where she and her theater friends congregated to sing and be gay on the occasions when she gave a party.

The kitchen was the biggest room in the house, containing a four-burner gas range and a medium-sized refrigerator, which Ulanova said she bought about seven years ago. The bathroom was of average size but unusual in that there were both shower and bath facilities.

"Well," said Ulanova, "is it what you expected?"

"It has been most interesting," I answered. But it had been much less sumptuous than I'd expected.

In political life Ulanova serves as deputy on the Moscow City Council. This, she said, meant many hours of letter writing and answering suggestions and complaints and long hours attending meetings. The Communist party, I thought to myself, had clearly taken care to see that this heroine of the Soviet Union was formally associated in a political role with the Soviet dictatorship.

But how politically conscious was Ulanova? Did she really believe the party doctrine of any means to an end?

I asked a couple of questions to draw her out.

"Are you an intensive student of Marx and Lenin?"

"Well, of course all Soviet children read Marx and Lenin. Their works comprise the principles by which this country is governed," she answered.

But as a government official you must have special knowledge of communist theory?"

"Well, I have read Marx and Lenin. Some of it, you know, is very technical, rather difficult reading."

I had clearly not gotten very far.

Before taking my leave I asked, "And if you had it to do over again would you choose the same profession?"

"Ah, who knows?" she said. "Perhaps I would become an electrical engineer. I like mechanical gadgets. I like to take things apart—radios and such—and put them back together again. It would be an easy profession for me."

As I reflected later on this unpretentious woman, so out of place, it seemed to me, in the land of secret police and concentration camps, I decided that Ulanova had somehow become a kind of artistic princess who could use the world of ballet and her own exalted place in it to separate her from the realities—at least to a greater degree than was possible for any other Russian.

And yet in police state Russia no one can truly stay separated from the realities very long. I was dramatically reminded of this within an hour of leaving Ulanova's apartment. I had gone straight from there to Spasso House, the official residence of America's Ambassador, Charles Bohlen. The introductions were scarcely over and the cocktails were just being handed out when a special messenger arrived. The Russians had shot down another American plane in the Far East. The American crew was presumed lost.

Looking back, it seemed that this timing was typical. No important phase of my Russian trip was ever isolated for very long from the dominant reality of the cold war between the dictatorships and the rest of the world. This reality was present even when I went the next day to visit a Russian maternity home.

## CHAPTER SIX

## Babies for Bolshevism

I had not expected a maternity home to have any relation to politics and the cold war. Not even in Russia. But I was wrong. And although I had been fascinated by what I'd read of developments in Soviet medicine, I hadn't anticipated that my visit to a Moscow maternity home would be the most revealing single experience of Russian attitudes toward life. But it was.

In the case of the maternity home tour I have to admit that being a woman journalist was a distinct advantage. This was one time when the four male reporters in Moscow were barred from the story merely on grounds of sex.

There was an interpreter present at the hospital by request, for I was sure that my broken Russian would be no match for technical medical terms.

The director of the maternity home was a handsome graying woman of fifty years. Like most Russian women,

she wore no lipstick or make-up. She said she was married
and had two children. Her salary was 2,000 rubles a month.
When the doctor entered her administrative office, where
I was waiting, she was still in the mask and white cap and
gown she had been wearing in the operating room. Later,
when we toured the hospital, I also was required to put on
a cap and gown.

Medical care in Russia is free. But, as elsewhere, bureaucratic medicine involves much red tape, much waiting in
line at clinics, for shots, for prescriptions, for treatment.
For the average Russian there is no family doctor. It is
very impersonal medicine. In principle Soviet doctors do
pay house calls. But, from what I heard, it's not always
easy to persuade the doctor that his personal presence is
required. There are still a few doctors who do some private
practice. A Russian can go to a private doctor if he has
the money.

In maternity cases pregnant women are supposed to
report to the clinic in their city district. According to the
Soviet doctor, it is rare except in emergencies that women
living in the big cities give birth at home rather than at
the maternity hospital. Working women are excused from
their jobs, with pay, thirty-five days before the birth of the
child and are required to be back on the job forty-five days
after the confinement. If the work is of a heavy nature,
the pregnant woman can ask to be transferred to an easier
job.

The Russian doctor said that in the early stages of preg-
nancy the woman is told to check in to the clinic once a
month, later once a week. A complete case history is kept,

the doctor added, including data on blood type, past diseases, and pelvic measurements.

I had received a special request from a woman's magazine to check Russian attitudes toward contraception. I found myself somewhat embarrassed at bringing up the matter, but when I did so the Russian lady doctor seemed unsurprised and answered in a matter-of-fact way.

I began this way: "I have noted the government's efforts to spur big families through medals, banners, and money inducements for mothers producing many children. Does this mean that contraceptives are hard to obtain?"

"No," the doctor answered, "we give information on contraceptives and they are available in the drugstores. But actually here in Russia most couples start using contraceptives only after they have had a number of children."

"What kind are in use?"

"From what I've read in your American medical journals," she replied, "our contraceptives are similar to those used in the West."

The maternity home had a capacity of 150 beds. Before we began our tour, the doctor told me about the system of painless childbirth which the Russians claim (falsely, I'm told) to have been the first to develop. The idea is pretty much the same as what in England and America goes under the title "natural childbirth."

"It is a matter in great part of psychology," the doctor said. "When told exactly what's going to happen, a mother —especially a mother bearing her first child—is less likely to develop a sense of panic. That is why we give them lectures on the exact processes of childbirth and how best to get the baby born with least difficulty. We also prescribe a routine of exercises for the mothers to practice so as to condition the muscles for the effort of childbirth."

"Do those who decide to try the painless childbirth system agree to do without anesthetic?" I asked.

"Yes," replied the doctor.

"What percentage do end up having their babies without anesthetic?"

"More than ninety-five per cent," she said.

"What kind of anesthetic do you use when it's necessary?"

"Belladonna and things like that. Also various gases and derivatives of ether."

"But do any of the mothers change their minds in the middle of the process?"

"No," said the doctor. I couldn't help wondering to myself if her patients were ever given the chance to change their minds. I soon stopped wondering. For it became clear, to me at least, that they were not.

Advance knowledge and muscle training may be of great assistance in childbirth but even in Russia it doesn't by any means make it painless, as was eloquently attested by moans and groans that met us when the doctor showed me the labor room. There were four women reclining on the narrow hospital beds and I deduced from the roughness of their features and the stockiness of their builds that they were of the peasant class. Although their moans dwindled into grimaces when they saw I was a foreigner, there was no doubt they were suffering varying degrees of pain.

I was particularly concerned with a pock-marked young

woman who had been in labor two days. She was suffering from high blood pressure and must have been carrying an enormous baby. Never have I seen a belly so horribly swollen and distorted. Despite my determination to be objective this sight was something of an emotional and anesthetic shock. My reaction fortunately was not as sharp as that of the English schoolteacher, a member of an official British delegation, who, after visiting the maternity home, went back to Moscow's National Hotel and had hysterics in the lobby.

Before leaving the labor room I asked the pock-marked girl, "How do you feel about anesthesia?" I half hoped, I think, that this might prompt some action, for she was clearly suffering terribly.

"Oh, I would like to try it," she said. Then glancing at the doctor who was standing by, frozen-faced, she added, "Some other time of course. Just to try it."

I admired her discipline.

From what I could see, the hospital had a scrubbed look although sheets and blankets were obviously in short supply, being worn from much washing and sometimes patched. The main operating room probably held the essential minimum only. It was much more poorly equipped than the delivery room for instance at Columbia Presbyterian Hospital in New York, where I had my baby. It was revealing, I thought, that there was no incubator at the hospital to take care of premature babies.

In Russia a husband is not allowed to see his wife and baby until he goes to the hospital to take his family home. This is on the eighth day after the baby's birth.

There are no private rooms. Wards hold from twelve to twenty beds. It was in one of the wards that I began to grasp the gap between Western and Russian attitudes in the matter of privacy. The first thing that made an impression on me was the reaction of one of the convalescing mothers when I asked how she would like a room of her own. As this was being translated a look of alarm came into her eyes.

"Oh, Doctor," she said in a tone of agitation, "please don't separate me from my friends."

"It was only a theoretical question," the doctor said soothingly.

Then turning to me, she said, "What you don't understand is that we Russians don't feel the same way as you seem to in the West."

Over and over again I was to have experiences which convinced me that the crowding together and lack of privacy so typical of Russian life is far less of a hardship than we Westerners imagine. In fact, only a few hours after my visit to the maternity home I encountered this Russian abhorrence of solitude in a person who would be the most likely to appreciate its merits. He was a poet, Anatoly Surov, then chairman of the Writers Union. Surov himself brought up the question in describing a trip he had made through Scandinavia and England during the summer.

"Do you know," he said, "that I rode on a train for nine hours and not a single soul spoke to me? It was terrible. Why, if that had been Russia everyone in the compartment would have been talking, exchanging toasts. By the time we had reached our destinations we would be pledging life-long friendship. We would exchange addresses and promise faithfully to write. No one ever would of course, but that isn't what counts."

It is my conclusion that the Russians hate being alone more than any other people with whom I am acquainted. I've wondered if this isn't partly the result of the vastness of their land, which acre per acre is probably the most sparsely settled of all Eurasia. East of Moscow, especially, each group of human beings is an oasis in a desert of emptiness. Also the rigor of police state life could be an explanation. People who are afraid need the solace of human companionship more desperately than those who are serene and secure. Perhaps most Russian men and women need the reassurance of human companionship to best the fears—and the melancholy—to which as a people they have historically been prone. Solitary confinement must have special terrors for the Russian soul.

To get back to the maternity home, there are also special reasons there why young mothers would much prefer the chatter and companionship of the hospital ward to the isolation of a room to themselves. The most obvious is that they are deprived during their convalescence of any visitors from outside, including, as I've mentioned, their husbands.

When I visited the ward, the women were finishing up their noon meal. It included a kind of bread and rice pudding and bright red watermelon, which looked ripe and good. They seemed contented, a condition almost universal among women who have produced healthy babies.

In the nursery I saw for the first time something I had heard about, the tight wrapping of the infants, papoose style, so that even their arms are immobilized. I had read that this tight confinement of the infant was an early cause for Russian frustrations, an interesting, if doubtful, opinion.

Whatever the lacks of the maternity home, medical service to Russian women is a great improvement over what existed in the days of the Czar. Logically there would have been improvements in any regime as Russia caught up with the twentieth century. Whatever sins the Soviet state commits against the minds and bodies of its political opponents, it is certainly doing a lot to produce continuing crops of healthy children.

As I was leaving the maternity home I still had the plight of the pock-marked girl in mind. Turning to the doctor, I said, "About the girl who had been in labor so long—if she doesn't deliver pretty soon won't you have to give her something? She seemed to be in great pain."

"I don't think so," said the doctor. "The pain will not interfere in the long run with her own health or that of the baby."

I felt suddenly as though I were at an animal breeding station. Production of the human species was being facilitated with aim of obtaining the best physical specimens at least cost to the state. Emotional involvements were a luxury that might bring about waste. Anesthesia would be given when it was medically required. Pain cost the state less than belladonna.

I brought the matter up later in the day with a young

British diplomat whom I met at one of the diplomatic receptions in Moscow. These receptions relieve the social tedium of life because they mark the few occasions when prominent Russians mingle with the rest of the ordinary diplomatic mortals. The Britisher had special interest in the maternity home because his wife had been sent to calm down the hysterical British woman delegate at the National Hotel.

"But don't you see," the British diplomat interrupted, "the Russians are being scientifically bred for a purpose. All the government's emphasis on good health and maternity homes fits the Communist purpose. Why have maternity homes had priority over decent housing? Because the investment in adequate childbearing facilities brings quicker net rewards in increased and healthy population than housing. They couldn't do both so they chose maternity homes. The Russian drive to expand its manpower is just as alarming as was Hitler's—and for the same reasons."

And then he told me of an exchange that had taken place between members of former British Labor Minister Clement Atlee's delegation and Russian officialdom during the delegation's visit to Moscow.

The subject of population came up at a diplomatic reception when Nikita S. Khrushchev, First Secretary of the Communist party, commented that Russia was a vast country and could absorb many more people.

"We intend to double our population in the next few years," Khrushchev said.

Standing near by was another prominent Russian, who overheard the remark and added, "And double it again."

Since the Russian population already totals more than 200 million, to "double the population" and "double it again" would bring the total in Russia to more than 800 million. It was not comforting to think of America's main competitor and opponent in the world having a population of this size. And as I walked down the dark halls of my hotel to my room I felt extremely depressed. But I was snapped out of it by the velocity of events—events typical of the way things happen in Russia.

It had been more than a week since I had first asked to go to Soviet Central Asia and Siberia. I had turned in my itinerary and gone over it with Intourist. They had raised a number of objections. For instance, I had desired to fly to Barnaul, Siberia, via Novosibirsk. But, Intourist said, Novosibirsk was a forbidden city. I would have to come back to Sverdlovsk. This was twenty-four hours' flying time out of the way. Then the director of Intourist at the Metropole, who was undoubtedly one of the most efficient Russian officials with whom foreigners in Moscow came in contact, said he'd see what he could do about letting me stay overnight in Novosibirsk provided I remained within the confines of the airport hotel. Finally he said that in principle this had been arranged.

"When may I leave?" I asked Intourist.

"Ah, that is up to the Foreign Office press section," was the reply.

"When may I leave?" I asked the Foreign Office press section.

"That is up to Intourist," the press section said.

And so it had gone back and forth for several days.

Perhaps we foreigners, having heard so many tales of Russian deviousness, tend to be overly suspicious. But, as happened so often during my trip in Russia, I began to get the feeling of a run-around.

This time my suspicions were baseless. When I reached my hotel room the phone was ringing. Intourist was on the line. It had been three days since I'd heard from them. And the last time I had talked with them I had been annoyed because of the lackadaisical fashion in which my travel request was being handled, as if it really did not matter if I went today or next year. But when I answered the phone it was just the other way around.

"We have been trying to reach you for several hours," said the Intourist girl accusingly.

"Well," I said, "I've been working. What is it?"

"Your papers have come through. You may leave at once. Please come downstairs and buy your ticket."

"When," I said, "is 'at once'?" This was eight o'clock in the evening.

"The plane leaves for Tashkent at 3 A.M. Our car will pick you up at 1:30 A.M."

I started to protest. Then I stopped myself. I had said it was urgent, hadn't I? There were five hours in which to pack and find a place to store some of the things I wanted to leave behind.

"I'll be ready," I answered.

It was just two minutes after three and the rain was pouring down hard when the two-motored Russian DC-3 roared off the runway at Moscow's Vnukovo Airport.

"I wonder how many Americans have traveled alone through Soviet Asia and Siberia?" I thought to myself. Then I took my pill. I'd figured I'd probably need something to make me go to sleep.

## CHAPTER SEVEN

## Travel, Coincidences, and the Soviet Police

If I'd known in advance that during my travels I'd be arrested sixteen times, I might never have left Moscow. That would have been a mistake. For I was lucky, amazingly lucky when you consider how another American woman, Mrs. Betty Sommerlatte, was later manhandled by the police during her detention. While I was being held and questioned by the Russian militia (as distinguished from the MVD and MCB, who are the political police) I was treated correctly and I was always released within a few hours. I would not want to relive the moments of anxiety while the question of my release was being debated. But my detentions were always educational. One can learn a lot by sitting around police stations talking to the militia, or even in talking to the other people in the police stations.

So far as direct surveillance is concerned, if anybody was following me I didn't see him. So I was spared this annoyance from which our diplomats still suffer. To this day military attachés in Moscow cannot travel anywhere without finding themselves with uninvited company, usually inconspicuous men in blue serge suits. This is the uniform of the political police when they are shadowing a suspect.

I'd heard so much about the way foreigners are shadowed that after boarding my plane I looked my fellow passengers over carefully. But I didn't see any conspicuously inconspicuous types that might fall into the category of Soviet "dicks." Among the more interesting passengers were some Uzbeks and three gentlemen from Turkestan wearing gigantic sheep's-wool hats. Also on board was an official Afghan delegation which was homeward (Kabul) bound. The delegation included the Minister of Agriculture and several cabinet ministers. They were not Communists. They had been invited to Moscow to be shown the agricultural exhibition and to be impressed—the Russians hoped—with the tall buildings and big factories of their Soviet neighbor. And those who had never been out of Afghanistan before *were* impressed. Most representatives of Asian nations find that Moscow is a pleasant contrast to the backwardness of their own countries. They have no real way of knowing that elsewhere, including the United States, there has been infinitely more progress than in Russia. What they see is that Russia, which is herself partly an Asian nation, has achieved industrial might literally amazing to an Afghanistan citizen.

On learning that the Afghans were on board the plane (they spoke some French and some German) I felt a great sense of relief. Perhaps it was the feeling that the Russians wouldn't dare do anything unpleasant so long as there was a foreign delegation around.

As the trip got under way, there were a number of surprises. I'd heard a lot of stories about how Russian airplane pilots skimmed treetops and took off without warming up their engines. Most of these stories dated from experiences of Americans during wartime or immediately thereafter. If my experience is typical, it is no longer true.

The pilot and copilot of the airplane, whose uniforms somewhat resembled the dark blue and gold braid of the American naval officer, were careful, competent men who evidently had been instructed to take every reasonable precaution. And as I traveled I was to conclude more and more that no matter what the country, the profession molds the personality into outlines that are internationally recognizable. For the manner and physical make-up of the Russian pilots was much the same as that of pilots anywhere in the world. After all, the requirements for being a flyer—sharp senses, above-average intelligence, emotional control, quick response—are the same in any country.

And a few days later when I saw some Russian photographers putting some Indian movie stars through their paces ("Will you move your purse to the right, *gaspasha* [lady]?" "Now act as if you are talking to each other . . . Hold it please for just one more.") I decided additionally that photographers everywhere in the world have just about the same degree of uninhibited aggressivness so far as the job is concerned.

For most of the trip our two-motored DC-3 flew at a conservative six thousand feet. The engines were always revved up before our departures. Seat belts are not used on Soviet planes but the "No Smoking" sign goes on during take-off and landing. Baggage is usually carried on the plane by the passenger himself if it is a small piece, and stored just behind the pilots' compartment.

The stewardess takes coats and bundles and distributes Russian magazines. No food is served on board but I'd been warned and brought a lunch. It consisted of cold chicken (by our standards Russian chickens are scrawny), several hard-boiled eggs, and some black bread. I always had to argue to get the black bread, for the Russians are developing their own snobbishness in this regard. Despite the fact that they have much of the vitamin content refined out of them, the lighter breads are becoming the favorites, and the only reason I can suggest for it is that the Russians think eating light bread is more elegant.

The only refreshment on a Russian plane is tea and that is served on request. The stewardess also had a liberal supply of chessboards. All the passengers, except the Afghans, played a game or two at some point in the trip.

Our plane, a frank copy of the American military C-47, or Dakota, was the only kind of passenger plane I saw functioning in Russia though I was told that there are a few three-motored types. It is rumored that the reason foreign airlines are not permitted to fly to Moscow is that the Soviet leadership doesn't want its people to realize that even small countries such as Holland and Belgium can afford four-motored civilian passenger planes, whereas gigantic Russia cannot. All four-motored planes in Russia are military.

It took us thirteen hours to fly from Moscow to Tashkent, with one stop at Aktyubinsk. There the waitress mistook me for a member of the Afghanistan delegation, or at least as a member of some foreign delegation. Since all official delegations are the guests of the Russian Government, I was offered a huge breakfast of hashed meat and potatoes and tomatoes that was on the house. And I ate it.

My only real moment of anxiety on the flight was the landing at Tashkent. I could see from my window that the dirt runway was strewn with rocks. As we bumped and scraped over the rocks, I thought that a flat tire was inevitable. But nothing happened.

Markov, who is "Mr. Intourist" in Tashkent, was at the airstrip to meet me, having driven his Pobeda car directly to the spot where the plane parked. He had on light, almost yellow trousers, yellowish beige shirt with short sleeves, and a straw hat. He was one of the two Russian men I'd seen outside of official circles wearing a handsome tie. The other exception was Anatoly Surov, the poet, who, being a Stalin prize winner (40,000 rubles), could afford it. Markov spoke good English. More important, he said he would help me with my Russian, which I'd been studying en route from Moscow.

As we drove away from the dusty field toward the city, I felt as though I were back in Persia. There were the whitewashed mud houses and women with bright swirling skirts. Many were wrapped in big veils, for much of Uzbekistan, of which Tashkent is the capital, is Moslem: the Tashkent Mosque was always jammed during the weekly service on Friday. Then came the new city. Block after block of old-style houses are being destroyed in the government efforts to bring in the new. There were three new theaters and one had an elaborate garden and playing fountain. There was also the same gingerbread architecture I had noted in Moscow. From the standpoint of quantity construction was impressive: miles of new concrete apartment houses, government buildings, and shops. But I much preferred the color and bedlam of the old city, where every street corner seemed to turn into an impromptu bazaar and children offered you a glistening emerald clump of grapes for *"telko odin rubl* [only a ruble]." There were also ripe peaches, apricots, and watermelons.

The hotel was adequate. Like almost everything in Russia at the time of my visit it was under *remont* (reconstruction), for a visible effort was being made to spruce up the country. I knew that Party Secretary Khrushchev had said that tourism to Russia would soon be opened on a limited scale and this was presumably the reason for some of the refurbishing. Also a number of official Asian delegations as well as a French delegation had already visited Tashkent.

Strangers were still a novelty though. I remember the effect I had on a woman who approached me while I was waiting for a taxi and started asking about the handembroidered bag which I was carrying and which I had purchased in Indo-China.

"How beautiful it is!" she said. "Did you buy it in Moscow?"

"No," I replied, "I bought it in Indo-China. Free Indo-China."

"Oh," she said, raising her eyebrows in surprise. "Are you French?"

"No, I'm an American."

"An American! Then you must be a member of the Communist party."

"No," I said again. "I'm here as a journalist."

"Well, it's a beautiful bag," she said, and hastily moved away.

Sometimes, because people in the provinces tend to look on Muscovites as Iowans look on New Yorkers, I in my finery (by Russian standards) was thought to be from Russia's big town. In the bazaar at Tashkent a strange man came up to me and lavishly praised my shoes—black open-toed suede shoes with medium heels.

"Where did you buy them?" he asked, to Markov's annoyance.

"New York City," I answered.

I never saw a more surprised Uzbek. I told him the shoes had cost about $9.00, unbelievably cheap to a Russian because he has to pay between $70 and $140 for a decent pair of shoes. And this high cost of shoes was one reason I wandered around Moscow in my open-toed pair. I was just too stubborn to pay such huge sums for footwear. I was also able truthfully to tell the Uzbek that my dress, a simple silk with a round white collar, had cost $18.95 (I'd gotten it on sale at Garfinckel's), which again is astonishingly cheap. Nowhere in Russia did I see a passable dress for less than 400 rubles ($100).

Because I was a foreigner I was given special privileges in Tashkent, as everywhere else. For one thing I was given a room all to myself. Ordinary Russians, even if they are perfect strangers, are housed four, five, or six to a hotel room. The plumbing in Tashkent was not for the finicky. As in many places in Asia, there are no toilet seats, merely holes in the ground with footrests on either side. I was, however, repelled at the sloppiness of Russian bathroom habits, but evidently in the Tashkent hotel the chambermaids were warned in advance about the fussiness of foreigners. Every time I headed toward the bathroom, a covey of maids scurried ahead of me. There was always much sweeping and mopping up before they'd let me in. And in fairness I have to say that while the bathroom in Tashkent left much to be desired the housekeeping in the hotel in Samarkand was excellent. So conditions varied from place to place.

After depositing me in the hotel Markov asked me my wishes in a tentative tone of voice. I could see that he hadn't the faintest idea how to treat this lone woman from the United States of America and wished that she'd stayed in Moscow and saved him the problem.

My wishes were to go to the theater in the evening, a collective farm the following day, and to take a train to Samarkand the second evening.

"But it will be impossible to make arrangements for the train on such short notice," Markov said.

"Now, Markov," I replied, "my schedule was very closely worked out by the director of Intourist in Moscow. I am scheduled to leave for Samarkand tomorrow. I'm sure you would not want to interfere with a program arranged by your superiors in Moscow."

"Oh dear," said Markov, "I will ask them at the station. I will see what I can do."

All three requests were filled. My only complaint against Intourist—a complaint renewed elsewhere in the Soviet Union—was Markov's attempt to keep me isolated from the average Russian. When I reached my room, for instance, Markov said, "If you tell me what you want for supper I'll have it sent to your room."

"Isn't there a restaurant here?"

"Yes," he said, "but it is under *remont.*"

"That doesn't matter to me. I had rather eat there than sit here in my room."

Markov kept insisting. But this time I won.

Restaurants in Russia are so crowded that there is no such thing as being seated by yourself. It delighted me. It meant that no matter where I sat I'd be associated with ordinary Russians picked at random. Intourist tried to prevent such casual contacts. Perhaps Intourist's attitude reflected the pervasive Russian inferiority complex, the feeling that the conduct of the average Russian would not measure up favorably in the eyes of a foreigner.

This restaurant, too, was jammed. Workingmen with open collars, Uzbeks with their picturesque clothes vied for the attention of the waitresses, who were dressed in black with white aprons. Small bottles of vodka stood on many of the tables, which were covered with white cloths (obviously not changed very often). Russian beer varies greatly in quality from locality to locality. In Tashkent it was good and a lot of it was being drunk. The favorite dishes seemed to be rice pilaff, fried pieces of beef with an egg on top, thick sausage and borscht. Enormous quantities of tomatoes and cucumbers were being consumed, as this was the harvest season. My standard order still was for chicken or beef *stroganoff* and tomato salad because they were the only supper-dish words I knew how to say in Russian. By the time I got to Siberia my vocabulary had expanded enough so I could have a little more variety.

At my table were seated a young couple. The girl had come from Moscow to take a job as a registrar at the hospital. The young man was studying to be an architect. I had brought my Russian-English dictionary to the table with me (a practice I followed throughout my trips). But it turned out that both the young people spoke German. They asked the questions I was to hear almost everywhere I went in the Soviet Union.

"Is it true that America wants war?"

My answer as always was that America did not want war and if there were a conflict it would be precipitated by aggressive acts of Russia's leadership.

They also asked such questions as, "Is it true that unemployment is growing?" and, "Do workers in Detroit sleep in the streets and sell apples in order to get food to live?"

There was no doubt of their interest in things American. And they were personally kind. For instance, when I unsuccessfully requested ice cream from the waitress the couple suggested taking me to a local ice cream parlor. I should have had the presence of mind to accept but I had a ticket to the local theater and was not quick-witted enough to act on the hunch that a talk with these two young Russians would be far more rewarding than being a passive spectator at the theater.

I was soon doubly angry with myself. For as I rose to leave the young man rose also and accompanied me a short distance. Then he said in German, "Tell the people of America that we will never forget what they did for us!" It was the first and only time any Russian *volunteered* something good about my country. I was so flabbergasted that I merely muttered, "Thank you! Thank you!" and hurried out. How I wish now that I had explored the ideas and feelings behind that unexpected remark.

The program at the theater consisted of a presentation of Uzbek folk dances and Uzbek folk songs. The theater itself was slightly larger than a Broadway playhouse, looking more like a new movie house. It was crowded.

I was struck by the resemblance of the Uzbek dancing to that of both India and Persia. The strange sideways head movements of India were constantly employed; bangles on the ankles and on the wrists were an integral part of the rhythmic accompaniment provided by a single drum, a kind of gigantic tambourine with deep tones. It was played by a man. Each of the dances acted out a story. One of them was about a frivolous girl who cared for nothing except fun until she saw the light and was taught to appreciate the merits of hard work.

The singing reminded me of some of the eerie Flamenco music I'd heard in Spain. It is Moorish in influence, and indeed almost all parts of the world close to the Mediterranean seem to have adopted modifications of this music with its cascades of strange high sounds, sometimes almost a kind of organized wailing. When sung, this music requires enormous muscular control.

I had walked alone to the theater, only two blocks from the hotel. In the warm September night I had passed throngs lolling in the streets, gazing at the fountain in front of the theater, which reflected rainbow colors from adroitly placed spotlights. I could not help contrasting the bright play of color and the squalid little shacks a few blocks away which housed many of the theatergoers. And I could see why the regime, which was not prepared yet to give its people decent places to live, had to put so much emphasis on the theater. For the Russians the theater is an emotional safety valve. In America families have endless diversions at home. There are gardens to be planted, trees to prune, basements to be made into playrooms, phonographs to play, television to watch, parties to be given, goldfish to be fed. The home is the focal point of life. But if you and your family occupy a living space the size of a small ship's cabin and are without the pleasures afforded by consumer goods, you must seek what recreation there is outside the home. So the workers have to be given palaces of culture—public gymnasiums, movies, gardens, and theaters. "Palaces of culture" are symptomatic of a land where even recreation is collective.

After I had returned to my hotel from the theater I collected my key from the administrator and started toward my room. Then I had an idea. Turning quickly, I went back to the desk and, under the pretext of asking about breakfast, I glanced at the ledger. Neatly written next to my name and room number was the time of my return to the hotel, as well as the time of my departure.

The system of Russian controls over foreigners is so thorough that it's really a waste of Russian gold to hire official "shadowers." For one thing, every foreigner who wants to travel must obtain a special Russian passport. Then before the trip the police in Moscow must obtain prior clearance from the police in the cities one intends to visit. The police in Tashkent, for instance, had to be told in advance when I would arrive, how long and where I would stay. The same with every other city. Then this clearance was stamped on my passport. The Russian police knew where I was at every moment.

Even though I never observed any shadows during my travels there were a number of remarkable coincidences by which the Russians could have kept a detailed account of my doings without resorting to the irritating and clumsy kind of surveillance characteristic of the Stalin era. The coincidences began on the train between Tashkent and historic Samarkand, the one-time home of Tamerlane, the great Mongol warrior. When I boarded the train I discovered that a Russian photographer happened to draw the upper berth in my compartment. When we arrived in Samarkand the same photographer "coincidentally" helped to obtain transportation to the hotel—a very difficult task.

At the hotel it turned out that the telegram allegedly sent by the Moscow Intourist office had not arrived. But the photographer was "coincidentally" on hand to talk the hotel director into giving me a special room all to myself even though the hotel was so crowded a dozen Russians had slept all night in the lobby.

When I emerged for breakfast the photographer was again "coincidentally" on hand. He proposed showing me the sights of Samarkand. It just so happened, the photographer said, that he was the official photographer for the Republic of Uzbekistan and had been assigned to do a photographic essay on the splendors of Samarkand. (Truly magnificent mausoleums inlaid with bright blue and gold tiles. Tamerlane also built observatories and mosques. They resembled some of the loveliest of the ancient Egyptian and Turkish architecture. Tamerlane was a descendant of Genghis Khan, and extended his power from the Volga to the Great Wall of China before his death in 1405. Tamerlane was also an enthusiastic patron of the arts and of astronomy.)

If I happened to be interested in archaeology, the Russian added, he just happened to have extra copies of an extraordinary photo showing the exhumation by Soviet archaeologists of Tamerlane's body. The exhumation had taken place in order to check whether the great Mongol conqueror was in fact lame. The answer, according to the Russian archaeologists, was yes.

In addition to giving me a copy of the photograph depicting a moment of historical and archaeological import, the photographer said he would be pleased to snap some pictures as we toured the city. I accepted. As I explained before, my attitude toward surveillance was that I was operating within the rules and had nothing to hide.

If the Russian photographer was there to report on my activities it was not my concern so long as he did not interfere with what I wanted to do. He didn't. In fairness I must say that my suspicions concerning the photographer may have been unfounded. There is no way of knowing. On the theory that he might have blundered into this association with a foreigner quite innocently I asked him several times, "Do you think it's wise or safe for you to spend so much time with an American?" He brushed the queries aside. His lack of fear could have been explained first by the fact that the farther you get from Moscow, the less frightened people seem to be of foreigners. Secondly, even the ordinary Russian knows that after the death of Stalin there had been a degree of change in the official attitude toward the foreigner. There was, of course, no decree saying, "From now on Russians may freely associate with strangers." But the Russian who has learned that his fate may hang on sudden change in the party line has learned to look carefully for every clue to such changes. And when he reads long articles in Pravda about the vast numbers of foreign delegations visiting Russia, he knows something new is up.

My self-appointed photographer-guide balked only once during our sojourn in Samarkand. This was when I wanted to join some Uzbek workers picnicking in the forest near the main Samarkand bazaar. They were broiling shashlik over a charcoal fire. I was very hungry.

I asked whether the Uzbeks might be willing to let us purchase some lamb in the bazaar and broil some for us.

"The hotel would be better," said the photographer.

Remembering my hotel breakfast—cold sausage, bread, and tea because there had been no eggs (for some reason eggs were not available until after 10 A.M. in this hotel)— I replied, "No, not the hotel. This would be much better. If you like, I'll ask the Uzbeks."

The Uzbeks not only said they would broil the meat for us but invited us to join their circle, making a place for us on their blankets and insisting that we share their vodka. At the bazaar, the lamb cost 14 rubles a portion or a skewer ($3.25 at the official rate of exchange). We ate with our fingers and I enjoyed it.

At first the Uzbeks maintained poker faces about the news, conveyed by the photographer, that I was an American correspondent. But under the warming effect of the vodka questions flowed.

"Are you a capitalist?" "Can a worker buy meat in America?" "Do the women in America do heavy work?" "Is there drunkenness in America?"

To this last my answer was that I suspected there was some drunkenness almost everywhere in the universe. But during my visit to Russia the government was carrying on a vigorous campaign against drunkenness so the population was particularly conscious of the subject.

Pretty soon someone proposed a toast—"to peace." I added, "Let's make it peace *and freedom*." There was no vocal assent, no change of expression. But everybody drank.

There were several other incidents which made my stay in Samarkand unforgettable. The first was a funeral.

I came upon it while wandering alone down the main

street of the new town. At this point the photographer, whom I shall call Igor, had gone off to clamber through some more of Tamerlane's mosques. I had had quite enough of this during the morning. Suddenly there was the steady, insistent blare of brass instruments. I turned the corner and looked squarely into the face of a dead child being carried in a small coffin. The coffin was being held at an angle by its two male bearers so that the passer-by could see its contents. The dead child looked like a doll in a box. Her gray cheeks had been rouged. A tiny crown, like those one sees on the angels in church, haloed her brown curls. Garlands were carried by the family, who marched slowly with the child down the center of the street. The band, made up mainly of horns, followed after. The mother had her face screwed up in a suppressed agony of pain—it would have been better if she had allowed herself to cry.

Thinking of the universality of grief, I wandered into the Park of Culture and Rest, where I was to meet the photographer. He was to take me to the park's open-air movie. A Czech film was playing. The movie theater offered a lesson in the universality of boredom. For as we waited the loudspeaker blared a long political commentary. I noted with interest that nobody—and I mean literally nobody—in the audience was paying the slightest attention. As far as my eye could travel over the wooden benches everyone in the audience was talking animatedly to his neighbor. But the moment the film came on conversation dissolved into attentive silence. This was one of many times I was to witness mass boredom toward repetitive political harangues. But I also came to realize that boredom was a luxury the Russian could allow himself only when he felt he would not get caught at it—as in a crowded movie theater. The Communist leadership, which harps so insistently on the term "activist," considers apathy its worst psychological enemy. Yet Soviet Communist propaganda is so long-winded and rigid it must be a bore even to those who concoct it. The Communist system beats itself. Because propagandists are so afraid of making a mistake, they will repeat the tried and true formulas rather than seek an innovation—which might bring political trouble.

The Czech movie was also boring. We left in the middle. Because I wanted to have a look at the local characters, Igor took me to a beer garden in the park. We were seated next to a truck driver. Pretty soon our table was completed by a man who identified himself as the director of one of the local collective farms. The truck driver was quite drunk. He embarrassed his countrymen by proposing a toast to Studebaker trucks, which he said he had driven during the war. Then he began muttering angrily at the waitress that *si chas* [right now] really meant *odin chas* [in one hour].

The collective farm director helped to keep things lively by being extremely rude. When he found out who I was he announced loudly that if it were not for the fact that every other seat was taken he certainly wouldn't be seen in the company of a capitalist from a country where helpless workers were exploited by greedy bosses. After a while I explained to him that I was really just a worker myself. And after a few beers we were drinking toasts to peace and friendship. Finally I took from my purse a little gold-colored metal vial of perfume which Lou Marx, the toy magnate, had given to the ladies at a party at Club Twenty-One in New York City and gave it to him to take home to his wife. He showed no proletarian inhibitions whatsoever in accepting this luxury item from capitalist America.

My trouble with the Soviet police began in earnest only after my purchase of a camera. As a plain non-photographing newspaperman my experiences were by comparison comparatively serene. It's true that many of my requests for interviews or visits to factories and farms were ignored or turned down. But this was negative difficulty.

If trouble had to occur, it was certainly fitting that it should begin in Siberia, which has a reputation for such things. Actually my Siberian detention was the briefest of all and the authorities there were quite conciliatory considering that I had absent-mindedly neglected to carry the proper documents.

Considering all the trouble it caused, the camera, Russian-manufactured, had a harmless-sounding name, Lubitel, meaning amateur. I purchased the camera with the rather reluctant cooperation of Mr. Markov, who kept saying that if I waited until the stores opened at 11 A.M. I'd miss my plane to Alma-Ata, which left at noon. But by having the Intourist car wait at the department store exit I was able not only to buy the camera but to go across the street to a portrait studio and try to get some basic instructions on how to use it. Incredible as it may sound, I had never snapped a picture in my life. So the Russian had a terrible time trying to explain such things as focus, speed, and aperature setting. Finally he simply set my camera at f8 and one fiftieth of a second, told me not to shoot except in bright sunlight and to keep my back to the sun. Then he sent me on my way. Despite the fact that I didn't know till I got back to Moscow that there was a distance factor to consider, the majority of the films turned out fine.

At the Univermag, or general department store in Tashkent, the camera was priced at 130 rubles, about $32. The camera was a simplified version of the German Rolleiflex. The mere fact that I could purchase a camera was a notable change from the Stalin era. Then a foreigner's possession of any kind of photographic apparatus—still or movie camera—was evidence of espionage and carried with it prospect of jail or expulsion or both. In Stalin's day the only place from which Americans in Russia could take pictures was the sanctuary of the United States Embassy.

The reason I had not brought a camera to Russia was that I'd heard a lot about the spy phobia connected with photography. I feared that if I tried to take pictures I'd arouse such antipathy that my primary work as a reporter would be handicapped. The Soviet Foreign Office promulgated the new regulations lifting the ban on photography some eight months before my arrival in the country. Nonetheless, other correspondents had told me that the liberalization of the government's attitude toward foreign photographers still remained in great part a paper improvement only. Still, even though many films were confiscated and others censored, it was possible for the first time since World War II for foreigners to send some photographs out, by mail and Wirephoto. By Russian standards this was progress. With photographs of Russia so valuable and so rare, it seemed worth while risking a few hours in a police station now and then in order to get them.

All this sounds a lot more matter of fact than any of us felt. I would be less than honest if I did not admit that each time I was arrested I was scared. There was always the possibility that the stay in the police station might be unpleasantly long. And just as in war you are likely to be most frightened the first time you are under shellfire, even though it may be a light shelling, so was I the most nervous the first of the sixteen times that a Soviet policeman tapped me on the shoulder and asked me please to come along to the station.

At the time I was standing outside the bazaar in Barnaul, Central Siberia. Barnaul is an old town in the Altai section of Siberia, the area near the Mongolian border. This part of Siberia consists of rolling, wood-covered hills and long valleys filled with wheat. Barnaul, like the rest of Russia, is undergoing a construction boom. It is a jolt to drive off Barnaul's muddy side streets, lined with crudely built log houses, and emerge on the main avenue, where concrete apartment houses of pink stucco exteriors are being constructed. Conspicuous in their newness, these buildings vie for attention with the new government and Communist party buildings, the latter being in a kind of neo-classical style replete with Roman pillars and other adornments reminiscent of Greece and Rome and totally unsuitable in Barnaul!

I chose to go to Barnaul first because it was one of the few areas in Siberia that was not off limits to foreign travel. Second, it was in the heart of the areas in which

virgin or previously unplowed lands were being opened up
for the development of agriculture under Communist party
head Nikita Khrushchev's grandiose plan for increasing
food production. Also Barnaul contained a museum pur-
porting to show the world's first steam engine, which the
Russians claimed to have invented.

Just a few blocks from the museum I had become one
of many interested spectators to a fist fight between two
Russian sailors and a Soviet militiaman. Although the
Russians are very much afraid of the secret police (the
plain-clothes section of the MVD and even of the uniformed
section of the MVD), they seem to feel on an equal plane
with the regular police. Individual Russians can often be
seen engaged in violent arguments with these militiamen
when the latter are, for instance, seeking to redirect traffic.
In the case of the fight the crowd was all on the side of the
sailors, both of whom were very drunk. Despite the fact that
the sailors were therefore somewhat disorganized, the
militiaman, who was armed but who never sought to use
his gun, was unable to get the gobs under control until
police reinforcements arrived.

With this excitement over, I proceeded several blocks to
the central market. Just outside the main enclosure I
snapped a picture of some peasants standing before a
curious wooden home looking strangely similar to some
elaborate old-fashioned houses I remembered from Oak-
land, California. As I was rewinding the film, a voice said,
*"Documenty, pashilsta."*

The request came from a tall, neatly tailored militiaman.
Along with the MVD and high-ranking army officers, the

militia are Russia's best-dressed men. As the militiaman
repeated his demand for documents, I started fumbling in
my purse. My state of mind was not improved by the
discovery that I had left my Soviet passport behind in my
hotel room. As I've explained, every foreigner in Russia
must carry a special Soviet passport in addition to his own
national passport.

When I admitted that I just didn't seem to have my
Soviet passport with me, the militiaman asked, "Are you
traveling alone?"

"Yes," I said, trying not to sound on the defensive. (In
other areas of the U.S.S.R. I found that the fact that I was
traveling alone also excited suspicion.)

"Why?" he retorted.

"Because I'm a newspaper reporter out to form my impressions of your country. I am not traveling as a tourist."

He said that I should please accompany him to the police
station.

On the way I remembered that in my American passport
it was clearly written in Russian script (as part of the
Soviet visa) that I was traveling as a journalist. At the
police station I showed the visa. The senior militiaman
said, "This is sufficient. You may go."

## CHAPTER EIGHT

## *"Greetings from Siberia"*

By the time I had nearly completed my three-week tour of Soviet Central Asia and Siberia, I felt in a position to hazard a few generalities about Soviet attitudes toward foreigners. Sitting in the brand-new airport hotel constructed in Novosibirsk, which is also one of Siberia's newest and most bustling cities, I jotted the following comments in my notebook:

"In Russia today the attitude of the ordinary Soviet citizen to the foreigner vacillates between suspicion and consuming curiosity. Curiosity usually wins out, especially when there is an opportunity for some kind of conversation that is purely coincidental and not likely to attract the attention of police. In my case, public restaurants, trains, buses, and parks have been likely places for such conversations. Taxi drivers in Russia are as garrulous as those in Brooklyn—once they get started.

"On this trip I have probably talked casually with several hundred Russians, have conversed at some length with perhaps a dozen. I believe I have been unusually fortunate, since in talking with me the average Soviet citizen required not only a certain amount of courage, but patience, due to my linguistic limitations. But the fact that I was trying very hard to learn the language was appreciated by most Russians and seemed to encourage them to be helpful.

"There isn't any doubt that the current degree of fraternization between the Soviet citizen and foreigners—a degree so limited that it would still be considered subnormal anywhere else in the world—is a change from Stalin's day, when merely being seen in the presence of a foreigner could mean arrest.

"It seems to me that talking to a foreigner carries for the Russian the excitement of learning about the forbidden, the same kind of excitement that makes people eager to read a book that has been banned. So once the initial barrier was broken and if the Russians were not scared off by learning I was an American (being fair-haired, I was frequently mistaken for a Balt, an East German, or a citizen of one of the other northern satellites), I usually was in for a thorough cross-examination."

I had come through my travels with considerable warmth of feeling for the little people of Russia, mixed sometimes with considerable irritation at such typical Russian traits as barefaced lying and total irresponsibility toward the pledged word. (If Khrushchev and company are sincerely

interested in buttering up certain foreigners, my recommen-
dation would be to impose a national fine on every Russian
who tells a stranger he will meet him at such and such a
time and place and then fails either to show up or offer
any explanation as to why he didn't show up.) And yet even
in this I was sometimes pleasantly surprised. For instance,
I had not really expected that Igor, the official Uzbekistan
photographer, would keep his promise to deliver the photos
he had taken of our tour of Samarkand.

We had flown back to Tashkent together on the early-
morning plane from Samarkand. The flight had been un-
eventful except in the beginning. For as we taxied down the
runway I saw to my right out the window what must have
amounted to more than fifty Soviet jet fighters, their wings
glinting in the sunlight. There was no secret about them;
they were right in public view. Still it was a strange feeling
to see for the first time on the ground the enemy planes
that I had so often glimpsed in the sky shooting at our side
during the war in Korea.

At the Tashkent Airport Igor had, in saying good-by,
sworn lifelong friendship and additionally had promised
to develop all the film taken during the trip in Samarkand
and bring it to my hotel that evening. Shortly after ten he
turned up not only with the films but with a bottle of
vodka and some caviar.

As he finally said farewell he asked two things. The first
was whether I would write to him and send him a copy of
the paper containing articles about the Soviet Union.

"I will do so," I replied, "provided that I feel confident

that this would be all right with the Soviet authorities. I would not want to get either you or myself in trouble on this score."

"Trouble?" he protested. "There would be no trouble. We can read what we like."

This remark, being so flagrantly untrue, almost made me ask Igor bluntly if he was working for the secret police. But I thought, "What difference does it make now?" and refrained.

His second request was for some kind of souvenir of our acquaintance. I offered him a lovely scarf I had bought in New Delhi, suggesting that it would make a fine gift for his wife. But he wasn't interested. He had shown some curiosity about a little gold cloth zipper case in which I carried my jewelry. I offered this to him rather hoping he wouldn't accept, because it posed a problem as to what to do with a jade necklace which I had broken accidentally. But accept he did, and so the broken jewelry went into some sturdy envelopes I happened to have along. He also asked if he could have an ordinary comb made of tortoise shell which I had bought in Finland.

Why did he want the souvenirs? Did he want them to prove to the secret police that he had faithfully kept watch over the American journalist? Or did he really want sentimental souvenirs? It's anybody's guess.

Among the most vivid of my memories of Soviet Central Asia was the hospitality extended by the cotton collective 'Stalina" near Tashkent.

The scene again reminded me of Persia. The homes were

of whitewashed clay and were hidden from the dirt road by high walls. Water, terribly scarce in this part of the world, was guided past the houses in open drains. The grape arbors, which served the families as outdoor rooms most of the year, often had to be watered by hand. Inside the collective farm homes there was no furniture to speak of, a characteristic of much of the Orient. But the floors were strewn with thick and beautiful rugs.

Cooking facilities were primitive. A grill was placed over a wood fire in special pits built under a shed in the far corner of the yard. But as I smelled the wonderful Uzbek bread being baked and caught the aroma of broiling lamb, I could not help thinking that the idea of progress often remains in debate. Sometimes primitive ways are better. Even in America we have reverted to the open barbecue. Gas and electric fires may be convenient but no one would claim that either can give food the tang and texture it gets when cooked over an open fire.

As we sat in the open in the grape arbor eating bread and grapes one of the Uzbek schoolgirls whose classroom at the collective I had just visited came shyly into the garden. She bowed, made a set speech in Uzbek, and handed me a huge bouquet of flowers.

The chairman of the collective, a grizzled old Uzbek, beamed in pride. "When I was a child almost no one learned to read," he said. "My mother and father were illiterate. Now everybody goes to school."

"What else has changed for the better, in your opinion?" I asked.

He paused a minute, then said, "Before, if someone got sick he had to go to Tashkent to see the doctor. Now we have a doctor right here."

"But best of all," he continued, "are the machines. It used to be that we would chop the cotton in the hot sun— chop, chop, chop, all day. Enough to break your back. Now we have the machines."

"Don't you think there would have been changes even without the Revolution?"

"I owe everything to the Revolution," he said. Perhaps he personally did. The position as collective farm chairman is a highly coveted one. If anyone were to be an enthusiast of the Bolshevist system, it would be such an official. Collective farm leaders are supposed to be freely elected every two years. But I noted that every collective farm chairman I met, including this Uzbek, had been in office for more than thirty years.

By American standards most of the homes of the collective farmers would have spelled poverty. But Uzbekistan is almost tropical in its temperatures. People live in their gardens most of the year. Everywhere in the U.S.S.R. each collective farm family has about one third of a hectare on which it can raise its own food. Most collective farm families are now permitted to own as their own property one milk cow and two calves, a breeding pig, ten sheep, ten beehives, and as many geese, ducks, and chickens as they can raise. The food produced on this personal property can be disposed of by the family as it wishes.

While working on the collectively owned land the farmers are paid so much per work day and also receive a percentage of the produce grown on the collective property—if there is enough left over after compulsory deliveries to the state have been met. The average collective farmer, I was told, earned between 600 and 800 rubles a month (between $150 and $200).

In order to encourage the collective farmers to greater production the Soviet Union has recently reduced the percentage of crops that must be delivered to the state at low fixed prices, and offered the farmers other new incentives.

"Stalina" was the third collective farm I had visited. In comparison with those I'd seen previously this farm was not so intimately linked with the other two pillars of modern Soviet farming, the machine tractor station (a central pool of machinery, mainly tractors, which are assigned to the collective farms when the harvest is ready or plowing must be done) and the state farms (the experimental and breeding stations).

Still the collective system of agriculture has been in operation now for more than twenty years and is highly systematized, with one branch carefully meshed with the others. It seems to me that even if there were a revolt against Communism (and unfortunately I saw no signs whatsoever that this was a concrete possibility) it would seem difficult to undo very much of the collective farm system, or at any rate to undo it quickly. But under a free system I have no doubt that important modifications could be introduced that would stimulate production by catering to the peasant's independent spirit and his hunger for his own land.

As I left the collective farm laden down with the

chairman's gifts of grapes, I thought to myself that I could understand how a foreigner without knowledge of Russian history could be very impressed at outward progress: cotton-picking machines instead of tired hands and bent backs, schools instead of illiteracy. Foreigners might overlook an essential point. In Russia millions had to starve and be jailed when Stalin decided to force collectivization of farm property despite the opposition of the peasantry. To this day the largest police force per capita in the world has to be maintained in order to enforce the Communist dictatorship, of which the collective is an integral part. And yet in many other areas of the world far greater progress has been made without enslaving anybody.

Again there is the philosophic point, "What is progress?" Does literacy per se mean "progress"? Can we be sure it leads to greater knowledge? At the collective farm literacy had facilitated everybody's ability to read the lies—such plain, unvarnished lies as claims that America started the war in Korea—that are printed in *Pravda*. Is that really progress?

The two most unpleasant incidents of my Central Asian and Siberian trip occurred in the town that was physically the most delightful. Alma-Ata, the capital of Kazakhstan, lies in a wide, fertile valley sheltered by high mountains. Because of the high altitudes there is excellent skiing and skating in winter. The Russians say they are going to turn Alma-Ata, which is very close to the Chinese border, into a kind of winter capital, a Russian Switzerland, so to speak. And in many ways the city, with its clean mountain air, its forests, streams, and lakes, was somewhat reminiscent of Switzerland. And so is the climate. It is the exhilarating kind that at harvest time produces wonderful crisp apples. So attractive is Alma-Ata that the native slant-eyed Kazakhs have been thoroughly outnumbered by European Russians, who, the Kazakhs complain, have taken over their capital. Alma-Ata even has a semi-Bohemian artistic set mostly made up of writers, dramatists, or intellectuals of one kind or another who found themselves in disfavor in Moscow as a result of swings in Communist party line on the correct approach to culture.

From the air the green of the Alma-Ata valley comes as a surprise. For the area between Tashkent and Alma-Ata is vast eroded desert, thousands and thousands of square miles of it. And any traveler who has traveled much by air in Russia and gazed at the high proportion of wasteland tends, as I did, to become much less awed thereafter at the bigness of Russia as it appears on the map.

I was greeted at the Alma-Ata Airport by a young English-speaking Russian boy who apparently was both an official greeter and passenger manager. As he accompanied me into the terminal he very politely inquired if there was anything he might do to assist me during my stay in the city.

"Why, yes," I replied, "there is one thing. Special arrangements were made in Moscow for me to fly to Novosibirsk on the early-morning flight leaving the thirteenth. I'd like to double-check my reservations."

A strange expression crossed his face. Then he said, "There are no flights to Novosibirsk on the date you mention. We are developing the virgin lands here, you see, and all the airplanes have been diverted to assist in transporting equipment and personnel. Therefore if you wish to go to Novosibirsk you will have to go to Sverdlovsk." (It would have been twenty-four hours to Sverdlovsk and then another twelve hours between Sverdlovsk and Novosibirsk, whereas between Alma-Ata and Novosibirsk the flight was less than seven hours.)

My first reaction was a feeling of defeat. I was exhausted already. And although I felt my trip to Russia would be incomplete if I didn't see Siberia, I questioned whether I should spend so much effort and time getting there. Then my despondency turned to anger. For I suddenly realized, intuitively if you like, that the young Russian was lying. And I knew why.

"You say there are no planes because you know Novosibirsk is supposed to be off limits to foreigners," I said accusingly. "But I've explained to you that the authorities in Moscow have specially cleared this with the police and arranged for me to go direct. Now will you please check my reservation?"

He went out of the room, but I'm sure it was just a ruse to convince me that he was looking into the matter.

For when he returned he repeated coldly, "The only planes available are those going to Tashkent and back to Moscow."

By the time I reached the hotel in Alma-Ata I was

feeling both furious and frustrated. My first act was to go
to the hotel director about the plane reservation. In Russia
most hotel directors are pretty high-ranking party members
as their job is considered to be highly sensitive. They are
also usually in the employ of the secret police. And while
this has its disadvantages it does give them unusual powers
which sometimes come in handy. At any rate, in my presence the director picked up the telephone and got to the
official who, I gathered, was the top boss. After the director
hung up he turned to me and said, "The airport director
knows all about your case. There is no problem. It has all
been arranged. You will leave at 6 A.M. the morning of the
thirteenth."

My reaction was a mixture of relief and of renewed out-
rage that the young airport official's lies should have caused
me such unnecessary anxiety.

Unfortunately for the young Russian, he was again on
duty the morning of my departure. Looking rather embarrassed, he asked if I would like to wait for my plane in the
rather plush sanctuary of the airport director's office. I
refused.

"What is the matter?" he asked.

That question was his mistake. My irritation was probably a matter of timing. The lies he had told me on the
morning of my arrival were the last of a long string which
various Russians in official places had been handing me
and I was sick of it. As a result I'm afraid I gave the young
man a loud and extremely pointed scolding on the question
of truthtelling.

"The matter is," I remember saying, "that I am not going to accept favors from someone who has deliberately lied to me."

"But I wasn't lying," he said. "There really wasn't any plane. This plane had to be arranged specially for you."

"Now you're telling another lie," I exploded. "I don't know how Russians feel when you lie to them but I know how foreigners feel. And if you are going to continue dealing with foreigners you had best learn to deal with them frankly. It would have been far better if you had simply told me that as far as you knew Novosibirsk was out of bounds to Westerners and that I would not be permitted on the plane. By telling such an obvious lie all you did is make a fool of yourself and bring discredit on your country."

I don't know whether my tirade had any effect on this Russian's conduct in the future. But I'm pretty sure I shook him at the time. For the only answer I got from him was an almost whispered *"Eezve neetye* [Excuse me]."

Perhaps it was Alma-Ata's invigorating atmosphere that provoked belligerence. At any rate, the night before my departure I had the most heated argument of my stay in Russia. It was with the hotel director, who, because the hotel dining room was under repair, volunteered to take me out to a local restaurant to dinner (but I paid the full check). I shall always remember him as the prototype of the blind total follower of Communism. His ranting monologue at the dinner table so annoyed and impressed me that I made extensive notes on it the moment I was alone.

Here are some excerpts: "In America you are capitalists.

You are exploiters of the people. I know all about it. When I was a child I worked twelve hours a day in a factory for a man whom I despised as one would despise a worm coming out of an apple. How I delighted in crushing that worm. In my childhood it was a struggle just to have bread on the table. Now I have bread and meat. I have all I need. My wife has a good job (doctor) and so do I. My sons have meat and bread and an education. I have built a three-room house. More is not necessary. I work for my country . . . I don't exploit anyone . . . I am not a capitalist."

The first time I interrupted him was when he said, "In your country if a member of the government marries a Jew he has to resign."

I straightened him out on that score rather vigorously. And he shifted his tack.

"Why do you not negotiate?" he asked. "Our government is willing to negotiate our problems. It is your government that always refuses. Why does your government object to the unification of Germany?"

I replied that our government was always ready to negotiate. So far as Germany is concerned, the United States stood for unification of the country provided the Russians would agree to elections, the freedom of which could be checked by inspection teams.

"Such inspection is not necessary," he said.

"Did it ever occur to you," I retorted, "that millions of people throughout the world do not trust the Soviet Union? Your government promised free and unfettered elections in

Poland, for instance. And I was in Poland at the time. The elections were a complete fraud and the Communists took power by trickery and by use of the police."

"We saved the Poles from Hitler," he said, "and they are better off than they were before."

There was a kind of question in his voice.

"Members of the Communist party may be slightly better off," I allowed.

'But you don't really think there is any comparison?"

"Well," I answered, "the Poles were able to get rid of the Hitler dictatorship. God knows whether and when they'll be able to get rid of the Communists."

It was stupid of me to have spoken so frankly, especially if I had any hopes of getting interviews with Russian officialdom. But I hadn't been able to help myself. I couldn't keep from laughing to myself when I contemplated the expression on the face of Mr. Simonov, the assistant chief of the press section, when he read the hotel director's report of this conversation as inserted in my dossier.

Most Americans who ask me about Siberia seem to envisage it as a vast wasteland dotted with barbed-wire fences, watch towers, and salt mines. And although my own preconceived notions were not that extreme I was rather surprised at the look of the countryside in the parts through which I traveled: Barnaul, Novosibirsk, Omsk, Sverdlovsk, and others. The real wastelands of Siberia are to the north and east, in places like Yakutsk, which is built on tundra and where scarcely anything will grow. As for the concentration camps, they are pretty inconspicuous in the more inhabited part of Siberia, though in Yakutsk and other regions the camps are the core around which cities are built since the camps provide most of the labor. But you don't have to go to Siberia to see prison labor at work. Right in Moscow's suburbs I have seen men and women herded to construction projects by Soviet tommy gunners who stand guard as the prisoners perform their tasks.

In South Central Siberia the land is patchworked with forests and an unexpectedly large proportion of it is under cultivation.

What surprised me about Novosibirsk were its modern buildings and the extensive number of new factories. We flew into the city on a bright, clear day and since we were flying low, I had a marvelously clear view, probably a better look than if I had been permitted to enter the town by car.

The city is cradled in the arms of the Ob River. The river is navigable: I could see ships being loaded at the docks. The buildings are sturdily constructed, mostly of stone and brick, undoubtedly as protection against the winter. I noted that there was an unusual number of multi-story buildings.

The airstrip on which we landed at Novosibirsk was dirt, but parallel to it a long concrete strip was just being completed. Novosibirsk is a main stop on the air route to Peking and that is one reason why the airport hotel, also newly completed, is so large. The Intourist representative was a young man of about twenty-one years. (On my stops in Central Asia and Siberia, Intourist was represented only at Tashkent and Novosibirsk.) He said that among the more prominent recent guests were the former Labor Prime Minister of England, Clement Atlee, Dame Edith Sitwell, and Aneurin Bevan, who rested in Novosibirsk overnight while en route to Peking.

"Dame Sitwell helped me with my English, which she said was far too Americanized," the young Russian confided.

It turned out that the Intourist guide was an avid language student. I happened to have along E. B. White's *Second Tree from the Corner,* which I'd brought along to cheer me up. I told him that Mr. White was one of the masters of English colloquial style and suggested he read a number of the short essays. He took the book gingerly, as if I were handing him a vial of explosive chemicals, and started to read. When the director of the Intourist restaurant entered the dining room, the young Russian hurriedly put the book down, and then seeing me look at him curiously, he paused a moment. The dilemma was real. Should he let the other Russian see him reading a possibly suspicious foreign book? But if he put the book down the American would understand that he was afraid. That wasn't good either. My reaction proved to be the lesser of the two evils. He handed me back the book, saying, "It would be nice to study some of the modern American writers. It is very difficult to get books like this."

I felt sorry for him. I could see that he was deeply embarrassed.

Of Siberian sights and sounds these are what I remember the most. First, there was the contrast between the freshly painted newness of Novosibirsk's airport and the old-fashioned look of the terminal at Barnaul, an hour's flying time away. At Barnaul as we touched down on the grass strip a horse-drawn wagon approached us. It was the baggage truck! The terminal building was merely a small house made of thick logs. In it was an iron stove. This was more like what I had expected of Siberia.

I also remember driving to one of the Siberian collective farms engaged in plowing up new lands, and seeing snow fall on the ripe golden wheat. It was September 12.

"It is unusual weather," the collective farm chairman said, "unusual even for Siberia."

"But what does make it so cold here?" I asked. "After all, Barnaul is very far south."

"Ah, but you see there are no high mountains anywhere in Central Siberia to shelter us from the Arctic. The Arctic winds blow straight across the land," he said.

I remember my surprise when my airplane touched down in Omsk and I saw standing on the strip several Russian helicopters. By their side were large military planes, probably jet bombers. Again there was no secret about them. They were there for all to see and the Soviet passengers were openly craning their necks to get a look at the big war planes. My surprise at seeing the helicopters was probably the result of subconscious disbelief that Russians were building them in any quantity. I'd seen Soviet photographs of such helicopters in their illustrated magazines. But I'd regarded them as just for show.

Of many conversations in this land by far the most interesting was with my Barnaul taxi driver, the one who drove me the sixty miles to the collective. He had been extremely quiet most of the day. Then on the way home he broke the silence. He was a rather vain, or at least uninhibited, person for he opened the conversation in an odd way.

"I dance extremely well," he said.

"Oh, you do?" I answered, wondering where this was leading. "What kind of music do you dance to?"

"Well, as a matter of fact, that's why I mentioned it," he said. "I am very fond of American music because it has such a nice steady rhythm."

This, of course, sharpened my interest. "Where in the world do you have the opportunity to hear American music?"

"Why, on my radio of course," he replied. "I get New York very clearly. Especially after midnight."

I was suspicious of this story. So I asked, "Well, what are some of the songs they are playing now in New York?"

As I mentioned, the taxi driver was quite uninhibited. And after thinking a minute he hummed in a rather pleasant tenor a song which I recognized to be "Young at Heart," which in fact was being played at the time in New York.

"Why, yes, I know that tune," I said. "You sing it very well."

"I know another one, a new hit in your country. Our orchestras in the *stolovayas* [restaurants] like it too." And once again he began to hum.

The "new hit" was "Melancholy Baby"!

When he had finished his rendition I asked if he also listened to Voice of America.

"I don't speak English. I only listen to the music," he replied.

The fact that he did not speak English was, of course, irrelevant as Voice of America is broadcast in Russian. However, that's all he would say in the matter. But now that the ice was broken he started to give me a real cross-examination on things in America—such a detailed cross-examination that I'm ashamed to say I had to guess at a lot of the answers.

Like many Russians he was particularly interested in unemployment, no doubt because of the fact that the Soviet press has grossly exaggerated current conditions in the United States. It paints lurid pictures of bread lines and homeless workers freezing in the streets, in fact the picture presented by the Russians is worse even than the terrible days of the depression.

"There's a lot of unemployment in your country, isn't there?" he said.

"There is *some* unemployment," I replied. "People aren't desperate or starving or anything like that."

"What do you mean?"

"Well, for one thing a great many Americans are covered by unemployment insurance," I explained. "Or they have private savings. Anyway, unemployment doesn't always signify that a person can't get a job. It sometimes means that he can't get the kind of a job he wants. For instance, I'm a journalist. I would be considered unem-ployed if I lost my job and would be entitled to receive money from the government for a certain period if I couldn't find a job in journalism. But even though I were classified as unemployed and drawing money from the government it still wouldn't mean that I couldn't find work of some kind. If it were a question of getting enough to eat I could become a sales clerk or a cook or a house-keeper. If you knew how desperate Americans are for household help you'd understand what I mean. If people were in need of money to buy food and clothing they'd be willing to take these household jobs. People aren't taking domestic jobs because they are holding out for something better and can afford to hold out."

Among the other things the cab driver wanted to know was the price of all my visible items of apparel. His curiosity was such that I think he'd have asked about more if he'd dared. Other typical questions: "How much does an American taxi driver earn?" (I estimated a minimum of forty dollars or fifty dollars a week.) "How much of an American worker's earnings go for rent?" (I estimated one fourth.) But I explained that the rest of the necessities of life—food, clothing, shoes—are so much cheaper in America than in Russia that the American worker ends up with far more necessities and luxuries of life than his Soviet counterpart.

This brought up the question of the price in the United States of a man's suit, of shoes, of a three-room house (my estimate was that you could get a small but decent four-room house in the suburbs for $6,000). And again, did Americans have television?

What interested me most was that despite Soviet propaganda about soaring inflation in America and the miserable lot of the U.S. worker, Russians were doubtful enough to make detailed inquiries of their own when they got the chance.

On my return trip to Moscow I had once again to pass through Novisibirsk. Even though I was still in Siberia I had a feeling of unreality that I had actually lived in and moved around this fabled and dreaded part of the world to which so many great and small men had been exiled. On the surface it had not been half as harsh as I'd expected. Yet even though I'd been there at an idyllic time of year, there had been snow on the golden grain. And although Barnaul was exciting and interesting to me because I was a stranger and everything was new, I could not forget the drunks sprawled on the dirt sidewalks of the side streets, or my conversation with the hotel barber, to whom I said, "Why do people drink so much in Barnaul?"

"What else is there to do?" he said.

An exaggeration perhaps. But in the land where snow tufts the grain in September and where cold shuts people up for most of the year, there *isn't* very much to do. Until the Russian Government can build the homes and heating systems to permit its people to defeat the weather, Siberia will have to be the home of the pioneers, the toughest of a tough race—or those who have no choice.

As I thought of these things, it suddenly occurred to me that there was no proof except my own word that I'd ever been in Siberia.

"Is there any way I can send a telegram?" I asked the Intourist representative.

"Where do you want to send it?" he said.

"Washington," I answered. "But what difference does

that make? Surely a big city like Novosibirsk can send a wire to any city in the United States?"

"What do you want to say?"

"Do you mean that whether or not I send the telegram depends on what I want to say?" I was feeling stubborn.

"Well, I'll have to ask," he said. He went in search of someone who turned out to be the airport director. The airport director called in a man in uniform. The man in uniform called somebody on the telephone. Another man in uniform turned up. Conferences were held. I was asked several times where I wanted to send the telegram even though I'd already carefully explained. Several hours went by.

I was about to board my plane when word came that I could indeed send the telegram. And that is how it came about that several of my friends in Washington, D.C., were awakened several days later at about 3 A.M. with a call from a somewhat baffled Western Union operator, who said, "I have a telegram here. It says—well, it says it comes from Siberia. Could that possibly be right?"

And the message that had caused all the conferences was: GREETINGS FROM SIBERIA. LOVE, MARGUERITE.

## CHAPTER NINE

*Russian Potpourri*

My first week back in Moscow was almost as eventful as the Siberian trip. After six days of negotiation that would have befitted an international conference I finally managed to get into the home of an ordinary Russian. I also interviewed some of Russia's top-flight sports stars, attended a fashion show, and had my first long conversation with a Russian of some importance. He was Andrei Gromyko, Deputy Foreign Minister.

I also began to understand a little of how Russians in the provinces feel about Moscow as the Big City. After two nights in a Barnaul hotel, where because of the unseasonal cold I had gone to bed with my polo coat on, and fifteen hours on the plane, the gleaming lights of Moscow seemed unusually bright. It was wonderful to be in a mild climate (compared with Siberia), have a room with bath and hot water, and talk to other Westerners again.

One of my first acts on returning to Moscow was to telephone Nadia to remind her of her promise to let me come to visit her. She sounded very matter-of-fact about the project and said she would come to tea at five o'clock the next day to talk it over. I began to feel slightly smug. The smugness disappeared quickly. For five o'clock came and went and Nadia did not show up.

I was advised to forget about it. I did. But the following day—and without a word of advance notice—Nadia turned up at my room in the Metropole. It was lunch time and I invited her to stay. She did. I waited for her to bring up the matter of visiting her home. When she kept silent, I decided that for a while I would not press the matter.

My friends among the Western correspondents said Nadia's behavior was typical of the Russians. Others added, "I told you so." But I wasn't quite licked yet.

During the same week Nadia and I went to a concert, a movie, and met for several more lunches. At this point I felt that we were well enough acquainted so that I could put things straight.

"I hope you'll forgive me for bringing the matter up again," I said. "But I do hate to return home without having some idea of how the average Muscovite lives. As I explained before, if I could visit your home without bringing you any difficulties I'd be grateful."

"Of course there are no difficulties," Nadia said firmly. "I had been planning to remind you of your visit myself. After all, we can do what we like with our personal lives. If you'd like to come to tea tomorrow, I'll come and fetch you at the hotel at five and we'll take a taxi over."

But she didn't turn up the next day. Or the five days after that. On the seventh day she telephoned to say her mother had been sick.

"But would you like to come to tea today?"

"Yes," I said. "Yes indeed."

Nadia's one room was located in a historic if dilapidated section of the city. It was five flights up in a block of apartments that had probably not seen paint since the Revolution. Outside the cobblestone street needed mending.

As we started up the stairs of the unlighted hall, Nadia appeared momentarily to hesitate. "Now you are going to write about how terribly we Russians live," she said. "You must remember that during the war many bombs fell and many buildings were destroyed."

I said I'd remember.

Nadia, who is thirty-four years old, is a war widow. Having no dependents and having no part in the Communist party hierarchy, she rated a low priority in housing. If housing had been available on the basis of ability to pay, Nadia could have afforded better, for she held down a good job as director of a photography shop. Her salary varied from 1,000 to 1,500 rubles a month, depending on whether or not she received bonuses. At the official dollar–ruble rate, Nadia's salary would equal $400 a month. But in terms of Soviet purchasing power it would be equivalent to $150.

The apartment in which Nadia lived was partitioned among five people: a childless couple, two single women in their thirties, and herself. The couple occupied what was originally the living room and a small dining alcove. Nadia's small room, which could not have been larger than six feet by ten feet, served as a combined living room-bedroom. She told me the other two women lived similarly. The rent unfurnished on Nadia's room was 20 rubles a month or $5.00 at the official rate of exchange.

They all shared the kitchen, which had an adequate-looking gas range with four burners. There was no icebox. The bathroom was old-fashioned but scrupulously clean.

Nadia had a sense both of neatness and décor. Her tiny room was cheerful because she had tacked up a kind of bright blue print material to serve as a "wall spread," matching the bedspread. The most impressive piece of furniture in the room was a big radio.

Nadia said she listened to both English and American broadcasts. She volunteered further that a Russian woman in the apartment building always listened to BBC for the purpose of improving her English, which she taught in a local high school.

Looking around the tiny austere room, I asked Nadia, "How do you spend your spare time?"

"Well, I must work very hard," she answered. "So I have little time. Often at night I am so exhausted I have little energy except to listen awhile to the radio, read a bit, and go to sleep. I like very much to read. There is a phonograph attached to the radio and I have quite a few records."

(The Russians have recently considerably increased their production of long-playing records. The record stores are jammed with both classical and jazz fans. The few electrical phonographs I saw in the stores were without automatic changers. The majority of the phonographs have wind-up mechanisms.)

"And," Nadia continued, "I have a mother and sister in Moscow. My sister is an engineer. Her husband also died during the war. My sister and I don't get along very well. I have always known how to sew and design and make nice things. And my mother always liked me the best. My sister is jealous and hot-tempered. But I am very fond of her boy. Almost every Sunday I try to take him on some kind of an outing.

"Then there are the movies and the ballet—when you can get tickets. But does this seem so meager then?"

I didn't say so. But it did seem infinitely meager. And yet Nadia's life had not been boring because she, like most Russians, had until the past few years constantly been stung by the needle of necessity. It had been such a struggle to live that there had been no time for ennui. Perhaps Russia's leadership was deliberately holding back some of the good things of life for this very reason. If Russians got decent homes, TV sets, and excellent food wouldn't they, being human, begin to develop a petit bourgeois philosophy? Wouldn't they want to stay home before the fire instead of attending the political rally at the local palace of culture? And from the point of view of the Russian leadership (nothing can stop the march of world Communism, says Molotov) such relaxation would undermine the drive to expand Communism and with it Soviet power. Such expansion of power requires energetic people, accustomed to struggle.

These were some of the thoughts that went through my head as I sat sipping tea in Nadia's tiny room and eating cookies topped with strawberry jam that her mother had made.

I never asked Nadia why she had failed to show up for six days in a row. I suspect that it was because she had to clear my visit with the police. I also suspect that she reported my visit and our subsequent meetings. Again, I was not disturbed. I had nothing to hide. And it's part of the peculiarity of life in Russia that there is no way of knowing just what the real reasons were.

In any event, being with Nadia was instructive because she was willing to discuss almost any subject. I remember talking to Nadia, for instance, about how the Russians arrive at their ideas of good and bad. In Western countries the Christian concepts such as the Ten Commandments, moral ideas of the Bible plus an admixture of the philosophies advanced by Plato, Aristotle, and others are bases of ethics. But officially the Soviet Union denounces everything about Christianity including, presumably, its ethics.

"It's very simple," Nadia had said in answer to my question. "What's good is what is good for the state."

"What about murder?" I asked. "Is it all right to commit murder if it's in the interest of the Soviet state?"

"No," said Nadia. "Murder is wrong. But Russians never commit murder in the interest of the Soviet state."

I hesitated for a moment, debating bringing up the testimony of former Russian officials in the MVD who described their own part in various murder and blackmail plots perpetrated by the secret police. Then I decided to let it go.

"And how do you decide what's good for the state?"

"Our leaders decide," Nadia said, "and we do what they say."

"What about the current campaign in the press against divorce?" I asked. "It must be a big change from the free-love theories of Lenin's day."

"Such theories of free love have been proven incorrect," Nadia said primly. "Public opinion in Russia does not care if a man and woman live together before marriage. But it strongly condemns a woman who tries to steal another woman's husband. Public opinion supports everything that holds a family together."

In Russia today couples seeking divorce must first go to a special counselor, who seeks to reconcile them. It is only when a reconciliation proves impossible that a divorce is granted.

Questions of ethics were also involved in my investigation of the Soviet sport picture. There is no doubt that the Russians are out to sweep the next Olympic games. But there is great argument in Western circles in Moscow as to just how ethical they will be in the process. It's an argument likely to rage long after the Olympics, for inexpert as I am in matters of athletics, I could see that there is great difficulty everywhere in defining exactly what constitutes an amateur.

Russian soccer teams would not, it seems to me, qualify as amateurs, for instance, though some Russian newsmen so described them in the fall of 1954, when they challenged and roundly beat the visiting British soccer team.

The Soviet director of the Dynamo Stadium himself told Western correspondents that the Soviet team are paid an average of 2,000 rubles a month in bonuses and that they get other special privileges.

Incidentally, on the night of the Dynamo-Arsenal match in Moscow's Dynamo Stadium (capacity more than 100,-000) a traffic jam occurred that would give pause to those who still scorn Soviet industrial potential. Cars were lined up four abreast and the creeping traffic line extended for miles. Special lanes had to be cleared to let the officials—and the teams—through. It took an hour and a half to make a journey that normally took ten minutes. It seemed that just about everybody in Moscow was headed for the sports stadium.

Even if Russia scrupulously followed every rule for amateur competition she would stand an excellent chance at the Olympics, because the developments of sports is government-supported and every facility is given its development on a mass basis. In America the development of sports is rather hit or miss and the number of participants is infinitely smaller, being voluntary, than in Russia. There a considerable amount of indirect compulsion is exercised to see to it that physical fitness is maintained, through mass gymnastics and other organized sports.

Sports competitions are organized at every level and in every facet of Soviet society—in the schools, in the trade unions, in political groups, in factories. Almost every Russian in a town of any size is given an opportunity to develop what sports ability, if any, he may have, and through constant competitions the best athletes emerge.

The picture above shows the vastness of Red Square and an enormous queue of people waiting to visit Stalin's tomb. The building with the star is one of the Kremlin towers, shown again below in this shot inside the Kremlin's walls, formerly forbidden territory.

*Note the contemplative look of the Uzbek tourist in Red Square as he eats ice cream and considers the quality of my ubiquitous $18.95 dress.*

*The entrance of my hotel, the Metropole, where the "Blue Hats," Russian security police, knocked at my door. At left is Galina Ulanova, Russia's prima ballerina, in costume.*

In front of Gum's, Moscow's largest department store, a uniformed Soviet schoolgirl contrasts my dress with that of the typical model in the window. The trees are reflected from Red Square.

A fashion show at one of Moscow's model houses. The model, unstylish by our standards, still contrasts markedly with the spectators, who queued up for hours to get in.

*Here is a picture, taken by the government's "official photographer," o the picnic with the Uzbeks in the Samarkand woods, and below is a grou of Uzbek youngsters playing a tambourine in the same forest near Tamer lane's tomb.*

This is the fabled Registand in Samarkand, the palace of Tamerlane, where
the Russians are restoring the beautiful mosaic work. Below is a closer
detail of the mosaic in its Central Square.

The blue tile mosaic glistens spectacularly in the sun in this Samarkand mosque where Tamerlane and his wives are buried. Below is old Samarkand's newly built market place. The semi-veiled woman, a common sight in Central Asia, reflects the Moslem influence. The mural is typical of the "look-how-happy-and-prosperous-we-Russians-are" school of painting.

Two Russians haggling over a watermelon in Alma-Ata, Kazakhstan's capital, near the Chinese border. This bazaar is a free market where collective farmers sell the food they grow. Below are some young Kazakhs in the market of Alma-Ata, which Russia hopes to make a Soviet Switzerland—but without ski lifts, "a soft and decadent bourgeois device," according to the ski official.

*The astonishing Party headquarters in Barnaul, Siberia, which contrasts strangely with Barnaul's log houses. The car is a Pobeda, about equivalent to 1930 Fords and Chevrolets. Below are peasants in Barnaul's market place, with an old wooden house in the background. Taking this picture produced the first of my sixteen detentions by Soviet militiamen. September in Barnaul is cold.*

The entrance of my hotel, the Altai, in Barnaul, Siberia, where the room was clean but hot water had to be specially ordered. Below is the director of the Ulianova collective farm I visited in Central Siberia. A big shot by Russian standards, he is dressed a little shabbily by ours.

*Two of Russia's churches: above, the Catholic church of St. Louis in Moscow, and below, a small chapel being reconstructed in Zagorsk, seventy kilometers north of Moscow. The reconstruction of such monuments is part of Russia's new tourist trade program.*

*Contrasts in Zagorsk. Above is a shoemaker whose makeshift work tent, held up by a crutch, is one of the few remaining examples of Russia's private enterprise. I took the picture with my new Russian Lubitel camera, modeled on the Rolleiflex. Below is one of Zagorsk's new apartment houses loaded with television antennae. TV broadcasts are confined to areas within one hundred miles of the biggest cities.*

In Ukrainian Kharkov, an old man kibitzes a Red Army officer's park chess game. Below, in downtown Kharkov, a peasant's vegetable cart contrasts with the shiny streetcars and a modernistic new building in the background.

This typical poster in Kharkov shows a Soviet soldier telling the villain, Uncle Sam, "Don't you threaten us." Below is the front of a Kharkov department store. The woman is eating an ice cream cone.

Two pictures of Stalingrad that show the new architecture arising from the rubble—the Planetarium above and an apartment building below. The ruined building beyond the new apartments will be preserved as a memorial of the siege of Stalingrad.

Stalingrad school children followed me around as I took pictures. The steps in the background lead from the Main Square to the Volga. Below is another bazaar—in Rostov-on-Don—where the women have brought their surplus from private plots on the collective farms to sell for what they can get.

*Yalta is the big resort and vacation place of Russia. Above are some hikers and campers unloading from a truck, and below is a beach scene showing the bikini has migrated from the French Riviera to the Black Sea.*

With more than 200 million people to choose from the Soviet officials are very cocky about their Olympic chances. For one thing, they know that the Soviet sportsmen are going to work harder than most other nationalities. The Olympic competition is being propagandized inside the U.S.S.R. into a question of Russia's national honor. Moreover, there is the spur of fear because failure of any kind where Russia's international standing is concerned is not healthy for the individual concerned.

My interview with the Russian Olympic champion, Galina Zybina, the woman world record holder for the shot-put, helped me understand a great deal about the sports craze in the Soviet Union and about Russia's recent successes in international competitions. The most interesting thing Zybina said was that her practice time *daily* consisted of three hours. That's a lot for any amateur and shows how intensively Soviet sport stars go about the business of staying in the big league.

The first time this kind of training provided spectacular results was in the spring of 1954. In prior Olympic games the Russians had shown themselves to be a very definite challenge to the rest of the world. But it was at Berne, Switzerland, that the world really began to take astonished notice. At the All-European track and field meet there the Russians scored 269 points—two and a half times as many as the runner-up team, Great Britain. Only four years previously the Russians had made a mediocre showing at the same meet, for they had only just begun to turn their national attention to the fine arts of track and field competition.

At the Dynamo Stadium among those working out in the practice field were Vladimir Kuc, Soviet Army sportsman who has several times smashed the world record for the 5,000-meter run. Also present was Uri Lituyev, who in a match in London, October 13, 1954, took the 440-yard hurdle race in 51.3 seconds. This speed is three tenths of a second faster than the recognized world mark of 51.6 set by America's Charlie Moore in 1952.

Later while watching the athletes going through their paces, I asked the senior Russian coach how he accounted for Russia's recent successes.

"In the first place," he answered, "Russia offers lots of people to choose from. And in recent years the government has been making special efforts to encourage sports at all levels. All the big cities are building sports stadiums similar to this one. [The Dynamo Club and Stadium possesses, in addition to the football field and track facilities, elaborate gymnastic equipment, including special rooms for boxing, wrestling, and tumbling.] It is a great honor in the Soviet Union to be a sport champion. Our people try very hard."

What the trainer also did not say was that sports are about as non-political as anything can be in Russia and as such are a welcome diversion both to spectators and participants. The big sports clubs in Russia make a handsome profit. The demand for tickets to football (soccer) games, prize fights, and wrestling matches is always greater than the supply. Also very popular with the Russians are ice hockey, automobile and motorcycle racing, and skiing. There is no golf.

In sports the Russians have the benefit of being thorough

and, as I've mentioned, tough. They don't have a chance to get soft. Most of them don't ride in automobiles. They walk. With much of life in Russia still similar to that of frontier America, durability is a necessity.

Miss Zybina, who won her world record with a shot-put toss at Helsinki of 50 feet, 2.58 inches, touched on this point of durability in discussing Soviet sportswomen.

"I have carefully observed the women of the West in Switzerland and England," the Russian girl said, "and it seems to me some of the reason for our success is simply a question of basic structure. We Russians are more strongly built."

Zybina, who had interrupted her practice to speak with me, was warmly clad; there was an icy drizzle. She wore a turtle-neck sweater, matching blue wool exercise pants, ankle-high tennis shoes, and wool socks. Zybina was very tall, her hands as strong and big as those of a stalwart man. She wore bright red polish on her close-cut nails and it contrasted strangely with her mannish hands. The polish was badly chipped but it was the only bright nail polish I saw on any Russian woman. Zybina had naturally ash blond hair and her cheeks were flushed the bright strawberry pink that one often sees on very fair Scandinavians.

In replying to questions on her amateur status Zybina said that she was studying at a technical school to be an optician. Like that of all Russians who qualify for higher education, Zybina's schooling is paid for by the government. She said she worked intensively on her studies. However, it was clear that neither she nor any of the other sport stars had any difficulty getting free time for international competitions. (Lituyev, the hurdler, said he was a schoolteacher.)

According to Miss Zybina, the track and field team engaged in more than fourteen competitions between January and October 1954, and at least half were outside Moscow. This would legitimately raise the question, it seemed to me, of how effective a student, or army man or teacher, anyone could be if he were so often absent.

Zybina and the others denied that being sports stars meant any special rewards, like the assignment of better quarters than those available to the ordinary citizen in their occupations.

"I live with my mother and five brothers and sisters, as I always did," Zybina said.

The Russian athletes were also unanimous in claiming that the only money they received during the trips abroad was given as spending money to cover such things as the purchase of clothes.

My interview with the Soviet sportsmen and -women was a fortunate accident which occurred after many weeks during which repeated requests to the Soviet press section had been ignored. I encountered the sports stars because I had gone to the Dynamo Stadium to familiarize myself with the field on which the Dynamo-Arsenal match was to be played. In fact, that very morning the Soviet foreign press section had called to say an interview was impossible because Zybina, Kuc, and others *were out of town*. They were not only not *out* of town but when directly approached, very talkative. Perhaps that's why Soviet officialdom tries to keep them away from the press.

Another happening of note during this eventful week, and also one very much concerned with ethics, was the conversation in which for the first time I heard a Russian criticize his government. It was mild criticism, to be sure. But most Russians usually concentrate either on long eulogies of their country's accomplishments or long excuses for any defects (how long, I wondered, will Russia's leadership be able, in light of West Germany's amazing comeback, to hide behind war as an excuse for continuing shortages?), so even mild criticism was a surprise. I shan't describe the circumstances of the conversation in detail because they would, in any case, have to be disguised. I can say that the Russian involved was a worker of the lower-income group with whom I happened by accident to be associated at some length during a rail trip.

We were talking about comparative standards of living when I asked, "Were the Russian people very sad at the death of Stalin?"

He looked at me speculatively.

"*Ny ochen* [not very]," he finally said.

"Really?" I said, inflecting the comment into a question.

"There are things," he said, "for which we do not thank Stalin. My father was a high-ranking naval officer. During the purges in the late 1930s he was arrested. We never knew why. They came to the house, told him to get his things, and took him away. I was a baby. My mother, a schoolteacher, has heard not one word since."

"But," I asked, "don't the authorities let your father keep your mother posted as to his health? Supposing he died? Wouldn't she be notified?"

"There is no communication permitted whatsoever," the Russian said. "That is part of the punishment."

This conversation raised some questions I've never completely answered. How many stoical, even seemingly contented, Russians against whom I brushed every day might have similar bitter memories? The purges of the thirties took 8 to twelve million. Another 3 to 5 million died or were imprisoned during the forcible collectivization of the farm lands. How many of the Russians climbing on buses, waiting on tables, selling ice cream may have had brothers, sisters, fathers, cousins, grandmothers, or friends taken away in the night? How deep were the scars? Or, to avoid trouble, had the individuals who had been bruised but not directly hurt by the dictatorship rationalized the past away as a violent phase that would not reoccur—a phase that had best not be mentioned lest there come fresh trouble?

From a journalistic point of view the contrasts within Russia are startling. One hour you will be having a somber discussion about the terrors of the Soviet police system. The next you will be reporting on the lighter side of life as evidenced by a Soviet fashion show.

The first fashion show I witnessed was at the model house several blocks from my hotel. Judging from the long lines waiting at the door, Russian women are starved for information on style and how to dress. The biggest difference between East and West in fashion shows is that in Russia the girls modeling the designs come in three sizes— or rather widths—whereas in the West fashion models look to me as though they had never eaten a full meal in their lives.

The first Russian model was announced by the model-house fashion director as being the prototype for thin women (in America the size would equal a 12 or 14). The second model was a woman in her early thirties, showing what the Russians called "normal sizes" (in America this plump model would wear a size 18 or 20). The third was the real embodiment of the middle-age spread. She was realistically announced as the model of clothes for the stout. (She would certainly need the very largest sizes in any American store.) I thought this system of models, in fat, plump, and reasonably thin categories, extremely sensible. The Russians might as well be realistic about the fact that the basic structure of Soviet women just is generally heftier than that of Western women.

As the models walked down the long ramp jutting out from the stage, the fashion director, who wore a severely tailored pin-striped navy blue suit, always gave the name of the Russian creator of each design shown. There were some imaginative ideas, but the designers were handicapped by materials of dubious quality and harsh colors. So far as dress materials are concerned, the Russians need to do a lot of work on their color processing. But then it is only recently that the Soviet Government has taken more than a passing interest in the fashion industry.

The audience was as interesting as the show. Next to me was a shy middle-aged lady. She wore boots (anyone who walks through the muddy streets of the suburbs and even some sections of Moscow proper understands the Russian partiality for boots), cotton stockings, a straight wool skirt, a quilted and padded cotton jacket, and a white crocheted kerchief. She was obviously popeyed at what to her must have seemed the great elegance of the silks and satins. And the one evening gown that was modeled—a very ordinary affair of black crepe—really brought sighs of envy.

I have yet to see a Russian woman in evening dress except at formal receptions or unless the woman was a professional entertainer, such as a concert pianist. Evening clothes are considered by most Russians as too swank for a workers' state. They reek too much of the capitalist past. And if any Russian couple were to turn up at a party in evening attire they would not only be considered eccentric but suspect.

If there were any elegantly groomed women in Russia I did not meet them. I don't blame Russian women for ignoring most cosmetics. From what I saw of the lipsticks and what I smelled of the perfume, the women are better off in their natural state.

The majority of Russian women—including the wealthiest, such as the wives of high Communist party officials—wear their hair parted in the middle and pulled straight back, doing up the ends in various braid arrangements. These women with their hair done in braids looked far more attractive to me than those who had gone to a beauty parlor, of which there are only a few, perhaps less than a dozen, in Moscow. And the reason braids are more attractive than permanents is that the Russian permanent wave systems are still primitive. The women who emerge from the electric waving machines are likely to look frizzled and therefore terribly unnatural.

So far as I could discover, no Russian woman ever dieted for the purpose of getting thin. I was always being lectured by the servants at the Hotel Metropole or by the waiters and waitresses in various restaurants to the effect that I didn't eat enough. And yet all during my stay in Moscow I kept gaining weight. Even the younger Russian women are stockier on the average than the girls in America. The Russian women seem to take it as a matter of course that as the years go by they will become plumper and plumper. Their husbands seem to accept it too. In fact, it has been such a long struggle for the masses of Russians to get enough to eat that many Russian men seem to consider their women's plumpness a kind of public proof of the family's prosperity.

As I looked around the audience at the fashion show I decided that certainly the most attractive thing about Russia is the air of blooming good health of the young girls. And I attribute much of this to the black bread.

Andrei Gromyko is a suave-looking, self-assured Russian diplomat whom I would not like to combat at a game of chess. Gromyko became one of the first Russians to make it a practice at diplomatic receptions to make himself highly accessible to Western newsmen and to use the personal exchange to emphasize the current Soviet line.

I first met him in Moscow at a reception given by the American Ambassador for two visiting congressmen. Congressman Battle, who had sponsored the bill for limiting trade with Iron Curtain countries, was the butt of considerable sarcasm from Mr. Gromyko.

"Russia is greatly indebted to you for your trade activities," began Mr. Gromyko after introductions were over.

Mr. Battle, who is used to having people mean what they say instead of precisely the opposite, started to smile politely, thinking that Gromyko was about to launch into some diplomatic pleasantry.

Somebody warned him in time. "Gromyko's being sarcastic," a voice said from my side of the circle in which the congressman and Gromyko were at the moment the central figures.

And Gromyko was indeed being sarcastic. What he was trying to prove, it developed, was that America, in restricting East-West trade, had first made itself highly unpopular the world over, and secondly had messed up its own economy by making necessary the storage of huge surpluses of food, such as fats and grains.

"Do you mean to imply, Mr. Gromyko," an English correspondent queried, "that Russia would be interested in buying those surpluses stored in America?"

Mr. Gromyko merely shrugged his shoulders in a gesture that was beyond most of us.

I was about to dismiss the conversation as more meaningless talk when Mr. Gromyko turned to several of the correspondents and said suddenly, "I don't think the press has properly emphasized the recent great changes in Soviet policy, particularly the fact that we are now prepared to open up the country to inspection teams as part of atomic disarmament."

"Something along the line of the inspection teams in Korea?" I asked.

"The details are not worked out," Mr. Gromyko said, "but the point is that we have gone a long way to meet the West's position concerning inspection."

I had asked my question with wicked intent. For just before leaving Indo-China, where I had learned I would be sent to Russia, I had spoken at great length with a Swedish member of the armistice inspection team in Saigon. He had been passing through the Vietnamese capital on his way to Geneva and home. And the thesis he was going to try to sell the negotiators at Geneva was that in modern times *no system of inspection is enforceable* unless you have the good will of the other side, and that any agreement with the Communists relying on an inspection system as a safeguard would make the democracies vulnerable to a deal in which they would give up certain armaments without any guarantee that the enemy would do the same. He had pointed out that the international inspection team in Korea, made up of two Communists and two neutrals, had been stymied by its very composition. And even if the composition had been entirely of bona fide neutrals, the Swedish armistice commissioner said, the occupation authorities of the area to be inspected can always outwit the inspection team because they control the transportation. Unless Russia, for instance, were to abandon police state dictatorship, which provides for rigorous control of all foreigners, how could any kind of workable controls be devised?

This was the background to my next question.

"Mr. Gromyko, do you think that with the vastness of the United States and Russia, not to speak of China, Tibet, and other Communist controlled areas, anybody could rely on inspection teams? Wouldn't it be easy for any country to cheat if it wanted to?"

He shrugged his shoulders once again. "It is what your side wanted," he said.

But most of all he emphasized, as had the Chinese Ambassador at a reception a few nights earlier, Russia's desire to import certain goods and its resentment against restrictions on the flow of these goods.

Someone brought up Russia's pledge to assist China in building up its heavy industry and war potential. The discussion began to get sharper when one of the growing crowd around Gromyko said, "Then coexistence is really a device for getting the goods and heavy tools from the West to build up Chinese and Russian heavy industry, which is synonymous with war power?"

"Trade," said Mr. Gromyko, neatly evading the question (to give him credit perhaps he did not quite get the question), "is naturally a part of coexistence."

As we left the party the British correspondent said, "During the thirties British engineers and British factories worked to help the Russians develop their industry. After the war we sent them jets. That was the last time we were having coexistence. Wonder what Russia and China will be building next time if we send them the big tools of heavy industry? I have a darn good idea it won't be something we'd like."

I agreed with him.

## CHAPTER TEN

Yalta

I was able to go by automobile to Yalta and the Ukraine because of the generosity of the Reverend George Bissonette, a Catholic priest of the Assumptionist order, who loaned me his car and Kolya, his Russian driver. Father Bissonette was the only Western churchman in Moscow. He was sent to Moscow as a representative of the Assumptionist order under an exchange agreement made between the United States and Russia during the 1930s. Early in 1955 Father Bissonette was expelled from Russia in retaliation for the fact that the State Department would not extend the American visa of a visiting Russian Archbishop. This brusque Russian action was taken despite the fact that only a few months before Nikita Khrushchev, Communist party Secretary, had singled out Father Bissonette at a diplomatic reception and introduced him to some top Russian officials, saying, "The father is a fine man." It is one of the many examples of something that Americans find hard to understand: the Russians never let personal likes and dislikes interfere with anything they do. Father Bissonette's expulsion was deeply regretted by those who knew him. An openhearted, intelligent man, he was a favorite of the foreign set.

The loan of Father Bissonette's car gave me much more freedom of movement than would have been possible by train or plane. But it was also very expensive. We bought our gas at the newly built service stations that dot the Moscow-Yalta road at intervals of about three hours' driving time. Gasoline cost more than a dollar a gallon.

The two-lane highway connecting Moscow and Yalta is made of asphalt. The surface is smooth enough so that an American automobile can be driven at about fifty miles an hour, risking only an occasional bad bump. It was an adventure to travel in Father Bissonette's shiny blue American Chevrolet. Everywhere we stopped we drew curious crowds.

"What kind of a car is it?" they would chorus.

And as they gawked they would also, to Kolya's despair, slide their fingers over the glistening surface.

"*Kak Zeiss* [Like the Russian Zeiss]," they would say. I'd always make a point of interrupting to retort, "It is the Zeiss that is like the Chevrolet."

On that trip I gave a ride as far as Yalta to the British correspondent for the London *Daily Mail*. He was traveling about the country in real capitalist fashion, I thought. For he took an Intourist interpreter everywhere he went. When he flew from Yalta to Kiev, for instance, it meant double

airplane fare, double hotel accommodations, etc. The interpreter, Madame Lavrova, was an intelligent, polite, middle-
aged woman. She was one of the few Russians who admitted
to being a churchgoer. She was also a very ardent sup-
porter of the Communist regime.

The Russian woman was a good companion because she
was always ready for discussion, serious and not so serious.
Once, for instance, we got to talking about love.

"But Madame Lavrova," I said teasingly, "is it believed
in the Soviet Union that such an unpolitical emotion as
love really exists?"

"Why, I'm sure that love exists," she said, bridling.
"I'm sure that's what we human beings need the most."

And she launched into a lengthy story about a Russian
man who had been cold and cruel to his own daughter and
had not matured enough to feel love until the birth of his
granddaughter, whom he adored.

Madame Lavrova was especially useful as interpreter
and guide at Yalta because she was personally well acquainted with the area, having been Mrs. Winston Churchill's personal interpreter during the historic meeting
among Stalin, Roosevelt, and Churchill. It was through
Madame Lavrova's good offices that the British journalist
and I became the first Westerners to be allowed to visit the
Livadia Palace, where the conference was held.

Before making the trip we had heard much about crop
failures in the Ukraine, the rich black-earth section of
Russia through which we drove on our way south. To
investigate the effect on food supplies in small towns we
made a point of picking out eating places at random. The

quality of the food was not so good as in Moscow, which
was to be expected, but otherwise we could see very little
difference. The cheaper grades of meat, sausage, and stew
meats, were plentiful. And although the restaurants never
seemed to have fresh fruits, it was usually possible to order
some kind of green salad or tomatoes. There was no shortage of bread—or of stout men and women.

The Ukraine is recognizable instantly by its rich earth.
The flat fields of dark loam stretch away from the eye,
forming, when they are plowed, an ocean of blackness. The
plowed ribbons seem to be visible for hundreds of miles,
disappearing finally into a very far horizon.

It takes thirteen hours to drive from Moscow to Kharkov,
the second-largest town in the Ukraine. When we pulled
into the Kharkov Intourist hotel we were weary folk.

Even though it was past midnight a Ukranian representative of Intourist was awaiting our arrival at the Kharkov
hotel. Our accommodations were clearly the hotel's best.
My room was distinguished by the presence of a grand
piano, which, while out of tune, was very imposing. The
hotel manager was very proud of his new lamps, which were
made of marble that had been fashioned into the form of
an owl. Orange light streamed through the slits in the owl's
eyes when the switch was turned on. And the curtains?
Red plush, of course.

Our priority aim in Kharkov was to visit the tractor factory. We had asked the Moscow press section in advance
to make arrangements by wire. To our surprise, everything
was in order.

The Kharkov plant operated on an assembly-line system,

turning out fifty-four new tractors a day. I am not an expert on machinery. But my British colleague, who specialized in economics, noted, to his considerable surprise, that the machinery was up-to-date and well cared for. The factory, in his opinion, was efficient. It was supposed to be one of the best-run factories in the Soviet Union. The management was especially proud of the inspection system, whereby each stage of production was checked so as to make sure no faulty parts got into the finished product.

Instead of being paid by the hour workers in this plant and in most of Russia are paid according to how much they produce. The technical term is piecework. If you sew one hundred buttons one work day but sew two hundred the next, your pay doubles.

The Communists call it "socialist competition" but in actuality they resort to the same kind of appeals to personal self-interest that are prevalent in other areas of the world. But the Russian system of penalties for doing a bad job is much different from that in the rest of the world. In America the worst that can happen to a man if he is persistently late on the job is to be fired. In Russia the worker who shows up late can be charged with a crime against the state and dispatched to a concentration camp.

An example of how the incentive system works in Russia was the case of Sergei Kuznetsov, a foreman at the tractor factory. Kuznetsov had become a hero of labor because he had developed a way of reboring certain pieces of machinery so that the same metal could be used twice. According to the plant director, this idea had saved the tractor plant 1.8 million rubles over a two-year period. Mr.

Kuznetsov had gone to the trouble of thinking up this economy because of factory policy of giving the originator of any money-saving idea a percentage of the factory's savings. Mr. Kuznetsov had received 30,000 rubles.

"What are you going to do with your money?" I asked.

"I am looking for a car," he said, "and I have moved my wife and family into an apartment in which we have our own individual kitchen. More is not necessary."

The director of the factory told us that more than one thousand money-saving suggestions had been turned in during September. Only a few had been accepted as practicable. But it showed how even in Russia the profit motive can spur the average worker to new ideas. When I said as much to the director, he said disapprovingly, "This has nothing to do with profits. That is for your Wall Street. This is socialist competition!" I concluded that all these terms were just jargon that the director plainly didn't understand.

The Communists also appeal to the natural human wish to be esteemed by one's fellows. They make much of public recognition. On the bulletin board of every factory shop were portraits of workers festooned in ribbons. Some had received medals for producing more in less time. Others had composed slogans which the factory had adopted. Sometimes a special banner was given to an enitre work brigade (about a dozen workers) that had particularly distinguished itself. And sometimes an entire factory is given special award if its operation is particularly efficient. The Kharkov tractor plant had won such an efficiency banner. It was like the "E" pennant that in wartime America was awarded to exceptional defense plants. But in Russia all this is called "socialist incentive." Someday the Russians will probably claim that they invented human nature!

Our tour of the plant also gave us a look at "socialist criticism." For on one of the ribbon-festooned bulletin boards was a caricature of a plant manager showing him to be luxuriating in a huge office while factory workers were unhealthily crowded into small quarters where the roof was leaking.

"If this Mr. Sorochenko is such a bad manager why don't you fire him?" I asked.

"But it's too hard to train a good manager," the director said. "Mr. Sorochenko understands about the criticism. He will improve."

In the machine tool section of the factory I stopped to talk with a young blond girl tending a metal press. Her name was Maria Maikina. At first she was so shy that it was difficult to get her to answer questions. It developed that she was twenty-two years old, unmarried, and earned 900 rubles ($250) a month. Her stockings were of coarse silk, or perhaps rayon. She wore flat shoes, a plain black skirt, and a white cotton blouse.

Maria said she was going to night school to finish her high school education, which had been interrupted by illness (ten years of schooling are now required in Russia). Afterward she hoped to go to a technical school so that she might develop skills that would bring her a higher salary. Maria added that she was toying with the idea of becoming an engineer.

"And when you get all this money what are you going

to use it for?" I asked. "Do you have any special hobbies?"

"I like books," she replied. "I'd like to have my own library. And I wish I could afford nice clothes. I'd like to be able to buy three good dresses a year and a pull-over."

It was also the machine tool shop that produced the most entertaining event of our six-hour tour of the plant, which sprawled over many acres. As we hurried down the shop's middle aisle the British newspaperman called my attention to row after row of machines stamped, "War Finish. Made in Cincinnati," "War Finish. Made in Detroit," "War Finish. Made in Wilmington," etc. There were also many German-made machines. As we emerged from the shop I asked one of the Russian engineers escorting us whether the American-made machinery was still efficient.

"Oh, we don't have any American machinery any more," he said.

I let it go. But it was too much for the British newspaperman, who was tired, hungry (we had not been offered lunch), and exasperated.

"Look here, my good man," he said in the somewhat stuffy British way he assumed when he was crossed, "come with me a moment." He grasped the Russian by the arm and propelled him back in the direction of the American machines.

Following along, I saw the British newsman pointing to the American machine and repeating loudly, "Detroit, spelt D E T R O I T! The city of Detroit, my good fellow, is in the United States of America!"

"Oh, there may be a few American machines here after all," the Russian said. "I had forgotten."

Trudging back to the director's office for our final briefing, we could see scrawled outside the factory buildings the slogans of the hour: "Peaceful coexistence," "Long live the friendship of the great Soviet and Chinese peoples," "Fight the imperialist warmongers."

Inside the shops the framed portrait of the Chinese dictator Mao Tse-tung was often more prominently displayed than the portraits of Russian officials. Also prominently displayed were pictures of Khrushchev—which was to be expected as he was a Ukrainian by birth—Bulganin, Molotov, Mikoyan, Stalin, and Lenin. Pictures of Malenkov, who at the time was still Premier, were also on the walls but not so frequently as those of Lenin, Stalin, or even Mao Tse-tung.

The director introduced us to his deputy plant managers, most of whom had worked their way up from positions as foremen or even plain laborers. The Soviet Union, having announced its desire to beat the United States in industrial production, takes care to provide opportunities and incentives for skilled technicians and engineers. And most of the men at Kharkov tractor plant had been able to qualify for posts as managers by taking special courses in night schools or by taking special leave to go to technical universities. Such leaves are granted to workers who show particular skill and intelligence.

There is monetary incentive, too. Plant managers are much better paid than the workers. Being a plant director frequently means the assignment of a good apartment, even of an official car. But it is a nerve-racking assignment, for if a director fails the penalties are sure to be at least the concentration camp.

The factory's finances were briefly described. According to the director, the state planners assigned a minimum yearly target quota of tractors and tractor spare parts production. Several million rubles are advanced and agreement is reached on the price the factory will charge for its products. The factory is directed to make a profit or at least to break even. It had to produce enough tractors and spare parts (sale of course is guaranteed) to cover the 2-million-ruble advance. And every money-saving operation—more work in less time, the invention of lavor-saving devices, methods of using the same tools twice—made the factory's financial position more secure. The director had the option of using any surplus profit for plant expansion, increased wages, bonuses, etc.

The Kharkov plant director had remarkably detailed answers to almost every question we put. His was supposed to be the best plant of its kind and he intended to keep it that way.

My last question was, "What concretely does peaceful coexistence mean to you as the director of a plant like this?"

"Why, for one thing," the director answered, "it would mean that we could import all the machine tools we want from places like England and America. The things we really need are on the restricted list, you know. And with the import of machine tools we could go into the tractor export business and beat the rest of the world at it."

I thought it was an honest answer.

On the way to Yalta the road twists and turns through mountains which drop away steeply to the sea. On reaching the Crimean sea resort it was as if one had come upon a proletarian Riviera where the inhabitants looked as if they had suddenly turned up after a hard day's work at the Brooklyn Navy Yard and hadn't had time to change their shirts. The appearance of the vacationers contrasted strikingly with the ornateness of the glistening white châteaux, villas, and hotels. Most had been built in the time of the Czars by the nobility, by the rich, and by well-to-do artists and writers.

To Westerners one of the more startling sights at Yalta's seaside boardwalk are the Russian vacationers strolling by in the kind of striped pajamas that in America are considered bedtime attire. I was less surprised than my British colleague for I had seen pajamas as hot-weather attire in Persia and China.

Yalta was vivid proof that despite Bolshevism a few Russians had managed to gain considerable riches. It was at Yalta that I first saw a family using one of the shiny black convertible Zeiss sedans. The women and children in the car looked very well dressed. The lady sitting in front was wearing the first really broad-brimmed picture hat I'd seen in Russia and had on a nicely cut silk dress.

The British correspondent and I were the first foreign correspondents permitted to visit Yalta since the second world war. This Crimean Riviera, with its green vineyards, soft sun, and refreshing blue waters, looked innocent enough of anything one might want to keep hidden from foreigners —on the surface.

But the Russian authorities had a guilty conscience about this area. It had once been the home of proud Chechen-Ingush tribes. After World War II, Stalin had ordered mass deportation to Siberia of these native tribes. They had been carted off in the middle of the night, truckload after truckload. Their crime had been that many had been friendly to the German armies. They preferred the German to the Bolshevik occupiers. In Stalin's deportations there had been no separation of the innocent from the guilty. If you had Chechen-Ingush blood, to Siberia you went.

By 1954 most of the once empty homes of the Chechen-Ingush families were peopled by European Russians. But Yalta remains mainly a resort area. The châteaux and big villas serve as rest homes (purely for recreation) or sanatoriums (where medical attention is available, and rest, recreation, and diet medically prescribed).

Russian workers obtain tickets to rest homes through their trade unions. As everybody now knows, the Soviet Trade Union in Russia really serves as the bureaucratic organization through which the lives of the workers are regulated. There is, of course, no such thing in the Soviet Union as the right to strike. Depending on the trade union and on the rest home, a thirty-day stay can cost a worker from 100 to 1,000 rubles. Transportation to and from the rest home is usually paid out of the worker's own pocket.

The first sanatorium we visited was the Livadia Palace, the site of the Big Three Yalta Conference. The palace is beautifully situated on one of the hillcrests framing Yalta harbor. We had a wonderful view of the hilly coast line studded with white houses and tropical vegetation and of the sun-flecked sea. The architecture of the white palace was simple in line. As we headed toward the main entrance I noted a ping-pong table, an outdoor dining area, lovely gardens dominated by fragrant pines, and the first ordinary Russian I had ever seen carrying a camera.

A young white-coated Russian doctor met us. At Madame Lavrova's request he agreed to take us through the sanatorium. In the open-air dining room edging the courtyard the vacationers were just finishing dessert, which consisted of lush green grapes.

Our guide showed us the high-ceilinged oak-paneled room where the conference had been held, an imposing place somewhat reminiscent of the great halls of the English castles. We passed through another large oak-paneled room that had been President Roosevelt's bedroom. On the second floor we were led to the suite once occupied by the late Czarina. We arrived during the afternoon rest period so we had to obtain special permission to enter this beautiful room with its magnificent large windows and commanding view of the hills and the sea.

Six Russian women occupied the room, in which as many hospital-sized beds had been placed. Although it's done, it's not an American idea of *fun* to share a room, no matter how beautiful, with five strangers. But again our concepts of privacy and those of the Russians are completely different. The sharing seemed to please these women, most of them factory workers. To them the Livadia Palace represented unprecedented luxury.

"Are you having a good time?" I asked the one who had identified herself as working in a Kharkov factory.

"It is wonderful," she said. "Before the Revolution this room belonged to the Czarina. Now even a factory worker like me can sleep in a room like this."

There was no denying the pride in her voice.

Yalta possessed the closest thing to a bar that I saw in Russia. It was a cubbyhole of a room on the main board-walk. An efficient and resourceful young woman dressed in white nurse-style uniform dispensed Caucasian wines and champagne, both dry and sweet, by the glass. I thought it typical of the strangeness of things in Russia that a big glass of champagne cost only 5 rubles ($1.25), which is less than it costs to buy two boiled eggs. Our first evening in Yalta we were in the bar (you sipped your drinks stand-ing up for there were no chairs) when I noticed the Russian woman sweeping the streets look in on us. Then she leaned her homemade broom against the wall, walked in, and ordered a drink. It was champagne.

Besides being a good vantage point from which to watch the Russian resort world, the bar provided interesting infor-mation about how Soviet barmaids handle drunks. When a very rambunctious drunk poked a stranger in the face and threatened disaster to the peaceful wine drinkers, the bar-maid rushed to the door and started blowing a whistle, especially provided, it seems, for that purpose. We noted that several of the waitresses at the restaurant down the block also rushed to the sidewalk and joined in the whistle chorus. It took three militiamen to get the drunk into a

jeep. The militiamen's job was not made any easier by the
fact that the crowd was unmistakably on the side of the
drunk, who received lusty cheers every time he broke from
a policeman's grasp.

We saw the drunk the next day—in the same bar. This
time he was painfully sober. He was accompanied by his
wife. A child of perhaps five years old held him by the
hand. What had the police done with him? They had taken
him to special center for handling drunks and let him sleep
it off. Then he had been taken home to his wife, who had
not been, we gathered, at all pleased with his performance.
The militia had evidently thought it punishment enough
to leave him in her custody.

He was in the bar in answer to his pleas that he needed
something to taper off with. He tapered off with *one* glass
of red wine. Then he went home, unprotestingly.


A small Russian orchestra played each evening at the
outdoor restaurant adjacent to our Yalta hotel. A favorite
song was "Besame Mucho" (later attacked by the Soviet
press as decadent and vulgar). Also frequently played (as
the Siberian cab driver had predicted) was "Melancholy
Baby." At one point we heard what we thought was a
Russian version of "Celery Stalks at Midnight." But the
Russian jazz beat is so staid that we couldn't be sure.

In Russia it is the custom for a man to wander from table
to table asking any girl present in the restaurant for a
dance. No formal introduction is required. I did a lot of
dancing. The Red Army officers were especially curious
about meeting an American girl. The Russians are at their

best in fast whirling waltzes. The fox trot rhythm is too bland, or perhaps too smooth, for their energetic tastes. A Russian fox trot, in my experience, is a kind of half walk, half waltz that is rather difficult to follow.

The only strained moment of the evening came when a rather elderly and belligerently drunk factory worker sat down at our table. He was full of denunciations of Western society, though I suspect a lot of this talk was for the benefit of two MVD or security police officers sitting at a nearby table.

"Why do you Americans think you are so superior?" the drunk repeated.

Then assuming the crafty look drunks often get, he tugged sharply at my arm.

"Would you ever consent to marry a Russian?" he asked.

"Of course I'd marry a Russian if I were in love with him," I said. Then I added, "Thousands and thousands of American girls are married to Russians, you know."

This caught his attention. "So?" he said. "How is that?"

"Well," I answered, "a lot of Russian refugees from Communism came to our country during the Revolution. Then after the second world war many Russians who had been brought to Germany as displaced persons decided they didn't want to go back to the Soviet Union. Instead they emigrated, many of them to the United States."

The drunk started to ask another question about Soviet emigrés. He first glanced over at the MVD men, who were staring intently at him. Then he thought better of it.

## CHAPTER ELEVEN

## Suspicion and Countersuspicion

By the time I was to leave Russia I had traveled more than 13,500 miles by train, automobile, and plane. As I reflected on what I had learned I was constantly reminded of how different are a reporter's methods of operation behind the Iron Curtain. The atmosphere in Russia caused all Western reporters in Moscow to exercise an extraordinary degree of self-censorship, not only in what we wrote but in the questions we asked. Often I blamed myself for having been too cautious, of letting fear inhibit me from driving hard enough to get the facts.

In a memo to my editors I summarized: "Russian suspiciousness and reputation for blackmail bring out in the foreigner a form of countersuspicion. In the case of foreign correspondents this results in a unique set of self-imposed restraints. No newsman can forget that reporters behind the

Iron Curtain have been condemned as spies for asking questions that would be routine anywhere else in the world."

Just before leaving Moscow for home I had a vivid experience that showed how these self-imposed inhibitions affect a newsman's performance. It was my encounter with the Blue Hats, as the Soviet security police (MVD) are described by foreigners because of the bright blue felt caps that they wear.

It was a Saturday afternoon about 3 P.M., lunch time around the Metropole Hotel. I had ordered my meal brought to my room by *perebuffet,* the Russian equivalent of room service. Because room service was usually so slow, I thought I had plenty of time for a bath before the meal arrived. But I was scarcely in the tub when there was a knock. Thinking this must be the speed record of the year for the *perebuffet* service, I slipped into my bathrobe and went to the door.

I opened it a crack. Outside stood two uniformed men in *blue hats.* I slammed the door shut.

I have often noted that reactions in time of danger can be wildly irrelevant. In my confusion I thought as I pulled my bathrobe around me, "Darn it, if I'm going to get arrested why do I have to suffer the indignity of not even being properly dressed?"

Then, with the door still closed, I started in my very imperfect Russian to ask questions. Being nervous, I made an important linguistic mistake. Instead of saying "*Shto vui hottitye* [What do you want]?" I said "*Kak vui hottitye* [How do you want]?"

This was greeted by a burst of giggles from the other

side of the door. Listening to the laughter, I thought to myself that this was obviously a very strange way for the dreaded Russian security police to behave. Then through the giggles which the uniformed men were attempting unsuccessfully to strangle, I heard the words "*Snakomi, snakomi* [Friend, friend]. Kiev, Kiev."

And suddenly it all became clear. These were not security police. They were air force officers, whose blue headgear somewhat resembled that of the security police. I had encountered the officers in a restaurant in Kiev, the capital of the Ukraine. The younger, who spoke a little English, had asked me and the British correspondent dining with me if he could pay us each a visit if he came to Moscow. We had each given him our Moscow addresses, never expecting to see him again. We felt that a Ukranian (Kiev was his home town) would be especially shy about calling on a foreigner located in a strange hotel in a strange city.

As soon as I had grasped the situation I told the Russian officers to wait a "*minutchkoo*" and hurriedly changed into a dress. When I admitted the officers they were each carrying a gift. The younger, a captain, had a box of candy from the Red October Candy Factory, which coincidentally I had visited the day before. The older, a colonel, carried a bottle of Russian cognac already well depleted.

But were these two air force officers genuinely out on the town to celebrate, as they said, the promotion of the younger from lieutenant to captain? Or had they been sent by the secret police? Were they perhaps going to try to stage a scene—two Russian officers alone with a girl—that could mean blackmail? Were the Russian headlines supposed to read, "American women seeks to pry military secrets out of Russian officers during drunken orgy?"

My countersuspicion was strong. I was far too vulnerable to take a chance. Before I admitted my two visitors I had telephoned Alexis Shiray, the Russian-speaking representative of the Agence France Presse and asked him to join us. And he finally did, so I had a witness. But was it coincidence that when Shiray asked my room number the Russian floor administrator insisted that I wasn't in?

I recall one particular phase of our conversation that sharply illustrates the psychological restraints of a foreign correspondent in Russia. This was when the captain volunteered the information that he and the colonel were going to fly in the aerial part of the parade celebrating the Bolshevik national holiday on November 7. Anyplace but behind the Iron Curtain, a reporter's natural response would be, "What kind of planes do you fly?" But if indeed this was a plant (and the unnerving thing is the uncertainty, for you can never know), any questions about airplanes could indeed be the basis for future charges of prying out military secrets. So I merely said, "Hmmm, interesting."

The Soviet captain added, "The colonel here has many decorations. He is a very brave man. He was a bomber pilot in Manchuria. He developed new techniques which even the Americans don't know about!"

"Hmmm," I said again.

"We often fly to Berlin these days," the bomber pilot interjected. "We can get there very fast in our new planes."

"They have interesting night clubs in Berlin," I said.

Then the bomber pilot began to get on more general topics. "Why do the Americans behave so badly toward our allies the Chinese?" he asked.

I told him that in America it was felt that it was the Chinese who were behaving badly toward us.

"But why are the Americans so unfriendly to us Russians?" the bomber pilot persisted. "What would happen if I were to visit America? Would I be stoned in the streets because I am a Soviet citizen?"

I told the bomber pilot that in my opinion he would be correctly treated if he came "*parahod* [by steamship]."

He got the point.

"Ah well," he said, "let us not talk about politics. Let's leave that to the politicians. After all, we are military men. It is not for us to bother with such things." (But this apolitical attitude is highly contrary to Communist wishes.)

The colonel, in addition to being an air hero, turned out to be something of a singer. After quite a few cognacs he got on the subject of some favorite cabaret personalities. At the prompting of the captain he volunteered to do some imitations. First he insisted on turning off all the main lights in the room. Then he sang and sang, mostly gypsy airs. Shiray, who could understand the words, said some of the imitations were quite good.

The colonel was a problem guest because he was so determined to get everybody drunk. He would fill up a water glass—yes a water glass!—and insist that the French correspondent and I drink it down, bottoms up. We did so once. Then we rebelled.

But the colonel protested it was nothing. "The best way is to drink without stopping, then bite into a lemon with sugar on it. That way you don't taste the brandy at all."

It was certainly obvious that it was only the effect, not the process of drinking, that the colonel craved.

Our evening with the Soviet Air Force officers ended on a gay note with the captain and the colonel extracting a promise from Shiray and myself to meet the following afternoon at 5:30 P.M. in my hotel room and to go out to dinner and the ballet. We agreed. But they didn't show up. We never saw them again.

Just the knowledge that your story is going to pass through censorship has a definite effect on the reporter. For one thing, instead of coming out and expressing himself straight and forcefully, he will try to figure how he can conceal his point from the censor and still get the story across to his editors. And in trying to get around censorship reporters have inadvertently written stories that end up by being misleading—especially if the editor at home does not understand that the point made in paragraph eight is really the hard news that you would like to have rewritten into the lead.

After Stalin's death there was some relaxation of censorship. Clifton Daniel of the New York *Times,* who arrived in Moscow at approximately the same time as I, was able to get much more through censorship than his predecessor, Harrison Salisbury.

My own experience with the censors had a rather amusing side to it. My first long piece described Soviet plans for expanding their tourist trade. The article said that the advent of tourism had been foreshadowed by several developments such as: 1. the construction of four new hotels, including one named the Ukraine, which according to Intourist was to have one thousand rooms and be the largest hotel in Europe; 2. extensive repair of historical monuments, including churches; 3. the fact that the Soviet chiefs of government have moved their personal quarters out of the Kremlin. Although the government offices remain in the ancient and historic fortress, a large number of buildings and churches inside its walls are being turned into museums that will be open to tourists; 4. the fact that foreigners are now allowed to take photographs.

My story added that the new regulations concerning photography were not always heeded, especially in the provinces, pointing out that I, for instance, had been arrested "some sixteen times" in the process of taking photographs.

The censor thought the story over for eighteen hours. Eventually it was passed with the deletion of but one word: sixteen. So the story reached New York saying that I was arrested some ——times. And my editors later reported that they had been highly amused at the cavalier manner in which I reported that sometimes I was arrested.

Matters of censorship are like much of the rest of life in Russia. It's like living by radar. You have to know the code. Words have a meaning quite different than in other parts of the world.

For instance, the Russians do not admit officially to having censorship. It is true that all copy must be submitted

through a little cubbyhole in the wall at the central tele-
graph office and frequently the carbon copy (returned
*after* the story is telegraphed so you have no way of warning
your editors) shows that paragraphs have been penciled
out. But you have agreed in advance to permit the Russians
to do this. Only it is not called "censorship." It is called
making "corrections." That is why every correspondent
must write at the bottom of every page he submits "corrections my risk."

Photography was undoubtedly the field in which self-
censorship was the most prevalent. For although no Westerner taking photographs has been detained for more than
a few hours, at least not recently, there is a definite psychological aftermath to police detention. The next time you
go out taking photographs you are likely to pass up many
a slightly unpleasant shot rather than risk getting into
difficulty with the militia. And this is so even though you
realize that according to the rules and regulations issued
by the Soviet Foreign Office you are technically within your
rights in taking the picture.

I am convinced that a certain amount of mild harassment
was part of the Soviet plan. The Soviet authorities must
have known such harassment would inspire considerable
restraint on the part of foreigners. Otherwise it would be
simple for the authorities, who have absolute control of
press, radio, posters, and television, to transmit to the
militia and Russian citizenry the instructions that foreigners
taking photographs are to be let alone.

As a precaution I always carried with me a Russian
translation of the rules governing the taking of photographs.

But even having it all down in black and white was sometimes not enough. My experience at Stalingrad was typical of how unpleasant the situation can sometimes get.

My difficulties began outside the bazaar or outdoor market place. I had with me my Lubitel and a movie camera with color film that I had borrowed in Moscow. My eye was caught by a bright display of succulent radishes presided over by a bright-eyed old lady whose graying hair was half concealed by a sky-blue kerchief. It seemed a good color shot and I started to film it. "Radishes," I thought to myself, "cannot by any stretch of the imagination be classified as war potential."

As I was filming the radishes a crowd gathered. Because cameras are still scarce in Russia mere possession of one arouses curiosity. Possessing *two* cameras makes people stop and ask questions: "What kind of camera are you using? Is it German? Why are you taking pictures?

Suddenly an MVD officer materialized at my elbow. This time he was genuine.

"Why are you taking pictures?" he asked.

Silently I handed him my Russian translation of the rules on photography. He looked them over quickly. Then speaking half to me and half to the crowd gathered around, he said, "Everything seems to be in order."

To get away from the curious crowd I retrieved my list of rules and regulations from the MVD officer and walked to the opposite end of the market place. There, as unobtrusively as I could, I started taking a picture of a vendor selling tomatoes, likewise scarcely to be classified as war potential.

This time the harassment came from an apparent civilian, a man in rumpled gray suit and golfer-style cap.

He, too, began by saying, "Why are you taking pictures?"

"I am an American newspaperwoman," I explained. (I always made a point of giving my nationality immediately. I did not want anyone to suggest that I was masquerading under another indentity. So far as the casual observer was concerned this would have been easy.)

"But you should not do that," the man in gray shouted, placing himself squarely in front of the camera. Then in a voice that could, it seemed to me, have reached clear to the Kremlin he began yelling, "Spy! Spy!"

It is extremely difficult to be inconspicuous with someone yelling, "Spy! Spy!" at you.

The crowd that gathered this time was big—and aggressive. When I tried to walk away they got ugly and pressed closer. A woman started grabbing at my cameras. For a time I could see no way out. Suddenly a militiaman appeared. If anyone had ever told me that the day would dawn when I'd be highly relieved at the sight of a Soviet policeman, I would not have believed him. But relieved I was.

So relieved that I took the trouble to settle the score with my shrieking tormentor. Before going off to the police station I turned on the gray-suited troublemaker with two phrases which I found very handy in my travels through Russia.

The first is *"Nye kulturni* [not cultured]." Now most Russians in the provinces have no real idea what "culture" is, but they know it's a disgrace to be without it. *Pravda*

tells them so every day. And if you really want to upset a
Russian, the most telling way is to use the phrase "*Nye
kulturni*."

The other handy word is "*piani*," which was easy for me
to remember because it sounds like piano. It means drunk,
and in modern Russia there are many occasions to employ
the word.

Addressing the gray-suited man, I began, "I am a
stranger in your country. It is very '*nye kulturni*' to behave
that way to a stranger, and furthermore I think you're
*piani*."

The crowd around the troublemaker thought my parting
words over for a moment. Deprived of me as a target, they
started instead abusing the gray-suited man. The last I
saw, men and women, including the one who had tried to
grab my camera, were shaking their fingers at him and
voices were chorusing, "*Nye kulturni! Vui piani!*"

The police station was a small wooden hut near the
bazaar. I showed my credentials and my Russian translation of the photography regulations.

"I have followed the instructions exactly," I said.

"Just a minute," said the militiaman.

It was three hours.

"Am I under arrest?" I asked at one point.

"Of course not," said the militiaman politely.

"Then am I free to leave?"

"Of course not," said the militiaman just as politely.

Finally after numerous telephone conversations the militiaman approached and said, "I'm sorry but you will have
to hand over your film."

"But it's the last film I have," I protested, adding, "You know very well that I have violated no rules."

"I'm sorry," said the militiaman.

Suddenly, on a hunch, I said, "Supposing I told you that I hadn't taken any photographs at all today?"

He knew, of course, that I had taken photographs. But he said, poker-faced, "Well, of course if you have taken no pictures it will not be necessary to take your film."

And he let me go.

There is no explaining it.

As for the man in the gray suit, he is inexplicable also. Was he an *agent provocateur,* a man deliberately instructed by the MVD to make life difficult for me? Or was he just a Russian who was victim of the spy phobia which Russia's leadership takes such care to instill into the people?

## CHAPTER TWELVE

## Stalin's Place in Post-Stalin Russia

Not long after Stalin's death General Bulganin, who was still Defense Minister, became one of the top Bolsheviks to make clear that many of Stalin's tactics in foreign policy would be discarded.

The future Premier did so in a conversation with a Turkish diplomat that created a sensation around Moscow because it was one of the first inklings of a change in line and because, under Stalin, relations with Turkey had been very strained.

In a conversational tête-à-tête General Bulganin emphasized strongly that Russia's new leadership was anxious to better relations with Turkey and specifically that Russia would no longer press for the Turkish provinces to which Stalin laid territorial claim.

The astonished Turk, who like most of his countrymen was extremely suspicious of the Russians, observed, "But Stalin seemed to attach great importance to those territories."

"Oh, that was just one of the aberrations of Stalin's old age," Bulganin said.

And this amazing irreverence toward the Soviet dictator soon was increasingly echoed in private conversation by other Soviet leaders.

The question of whether Stalin died a natural death or was murdered probably will be debated until the day—if it ever comes—that the Kremlin's secrets are bared to the world. But what is clear from the evidence is that many high-placed Russians, including some of Stalin's closest associates, were very glad to get rid of him.

For, as Bulganin intimated, Stalin in his last days was undoubtedly touched with senility. Probably because of his long training and reliance on intrigue and terror, senility, in Stalin's case, took the form of heightening his suspicion to the point of near insanity. It caused Russia's dictator to use terroristic tactics in ways so weird—even for Stalin—as to produce aberrations such as the anti-Semitic campaign culminating in the so-called "doctors' plot." In this plot nine physicians, most of them Jewish, were charged with the murder of the Soviet leader A. Zhdanov and with collaborating with American intelligence.

Stalin's terroristic plans were so irrational that not even his closest associates, not even Foreign Minister Molotov, one of the last of the prominent old Bolsheviks, could feel safe from the ax. In fact, Molotov did suffer a brutal blow.

For Stalin dispatched Madame Molotov to Siberia during the series of purges that erupted before the dictator died.

In January and February of 1953, the two months before Stalin's announced death, arrests and denunciations were increasing throughout the Soviet Union—Kiev, Sverdlovsk, Leningrad—at a tempo indicating a new and terrible nation-wide bloodletting. It is important to remember that these purges, which showed every sign of reaching into the Polit-buro itself (as had all previous large-scale purges), were interrupted only by Stalin's death. What a relief it must have been to Stalin's close associates—since not one could feel immune from danger—to have the threat removed in such a timely way.

Would Bulganin, who so quickly revealed his contempt for his former master, have survived? Would Khrushchev or Molotov? Nobody knows. But what is certain is that there were vast differences of opinion between these men and Stalin. No better proof is needed than the vigor with which the collective leadership set about undoing some of Stalin's last acts. One of the first and most dramatic moves of Stalin's heirs was the release of the nine Jewish doctors arrested on Stalin's orders. And it was publicly announced that there had been a miscarriage of justice.

Foreigners who have been in Russia during the successive reigns of Stalin, Georgi M. Malenkov, Bulganin, and Khrushchev say that the biggest difference between past and present is that the present leadership seems to tackle problems of government and power politics in a more rational way.

One of the most lucid summations on this score was given

to me by a veteran Asian diplomat in Moscow, who put it this way: "The horror of Stalin's last days—the days in which the new purge was clearly in the making—was that no Russian official or party worker knew where he stood. Under Stalin not even absolute unswerving loyalty was enough. You could obey all the rules and still be threatened. Stalin couldn't get used to the fact that he was no longer a revolutionary. He had resorted to so much terror and violence on the way up that even once at the top and firmly entrenched he couldn't get out of the habit.

"Now," the diplomat continued, "an attempt has been made to put things on a more rational, normal level. Don't mistake me. The Communist rules are just as strict as they ever were. Swift punishment is meted out to those who step over the political line. But at least Stalin's successors have made clear where the line is. Fear is still a powerful prod. Under Stalin it was fear of both the known *and* the unknown: the sudden arrest as a result of an inexplicable whim. Today the average Russian is more secure from whim. If he toes the line he has some assurance of being let alone."

The situation could change radically of course after— and if—Russia's leadership, dominated by Nikita Khrushchev, Communist party Secretary, can solidify power and with it the kind of authoritarian license that is available to the absolute dictator. As of early Fall 1955, Khrushchev was undoubtedly the "first among equals" in Russia's collective leadership. But should Khrushchev seek to move ahead to a position of unquestioned power, new purges would seem almost inevitable. After the Summit conference at Geneva, Western diplomats could find no sign that Khrushchev intended to push himself forward at the price of an internal upheaval at Russia's top levels.

In any event, it takes a certain passage of time even under an authoritarian system for the new leadership to entrench itself to the point of being able to act as it pleases without regard to feeling and advice of associates. It took nearly ten years of rule before Stalin felt himself secure enough to initiate the great purges of the 1930s, which ultimately sent to jail an estimated 8 to 12 million people.

There is a fascinating contrast of personality between the enigmatic, secretive Stalin and the bustling, extroverted Khrushchev, a balding, pudgy Ukranian endowed with awesome energy. Most striking are their respective attitudes toward public appearances. Stalin remained in virtual seclusion except for official dealings at the highest levels. He lived behind the fortress walls of the Kremlin. On the rare occasions when he emerged he was escorted by squads of shiny official cars that cleared the streets of traffic. Stalin's antipathy toward travel was deep-rooted. It was only after much stubborn persuasion that he consented to go as far as Teheran, Persia, to meet Roosevelt and Churchill.

Khrushchev, on the other hand, makes a great point of going out to meet the people. He turns up at collective farms in Siberia, inspects the latest agricultural fair in the Ukraine, and flies all the way to Peking, China, or Belgrade, Yugoslavia, personally to negotiate on foreign affairs.

Stalin was a formal man addicted to showy uniforms and the wearing of medals. Khrushchev is the epitome of the rumpled look and the impetuous gesture. He is even informal enough to drink so much that he has to be assisted to his limousine, as happened at a reception in Belgrade.

Stalin's place in history has and will experience many adjustments before it is finally fixed. Right after his death newspaper mentions of his name, which had often totaled hundreds in a single day, ceased altogether. After a time reference to Stalin reappeared in the press, but usually in company with Marx, Engels, and Lenin. For the moment Stalin's place in the hall of fame is definitely to be shared with previous Communist heroes. The special idolatry that surrounded him in his lifetime is gone.

It is symbolic of this attitude that although the incredible number of Stalin statues constructed in his last years are still standing, no new ones are being built. In the new parks of Soviet culture Stalin portraits hang alongside those of Lenin, Khrushchev, Voroshilov, and others. But now, as compared with the past, the portraits of Stalin are precisely the same size as that of the others.

Khrushchev's attitude toward Stalin since the dictator's death has been mixed. Stalin's theories and practices have been invoked when it suited Khrushchev's purposes and ignored and even repudiated when they did not. For instance, Khrushchev denounced the emphasis on consumer goods (slight as it was) during the brief reign as Premier of Georgi Malenkov on the grounds that this was anti-Stalinist and a betrayal of Communist dogma, which required emphasis on heavy industry.

But when it came to mending the break with Yugoslavia, Khrushchev was not inhibited in the slightest by the knowledge that it was the Stalinist line that had caused the trouble in the first place. In his abject apology for the incidents that led to the Cominform's ouster of Yugoslavia, Khrushchev went so far as to say, "We resolutely reject the things which occurred one after the other during that period."

(It was Stalin and Molotov who signed the letter resulting ultimately in Tito's expulsion. And it was Stalin's mouthpiece, the *Literary Gazette,* which said, "History will give Tito the choice of poison, as was Hitler's case, or the rope, as was Mussolini's case . . . The workers have long since discerned the vile and repulsive snout of the Belgrade deserter, hireling, spy and murderer, bankrupt fascist traitor.")

The best summation of Stalin's position in Russia today is that the dictator who let himself be deified in life has become just another Bolshevik leader whose memory will be revived when it suits current Soviet strategy. Death is probably the best protection for his reputation. For if he should indiscreetly come back to life today he would very likely be purged for his past blunders—such as the Yugoslavia affair.

## CHAPTER THIRTEEN

## *Some Comments on Bolshevik Manners and Morals*

If the United States Secretary of Health, Education and Welfare were to make a broadcast over the Voice of America berating Marilyn Monroe for divorcing Joe DiMaggio, these tactics would be roughly comparable to the way in which the Soviet state is seeking to enforce its current doctrines of Communist puritanism.

For in the campaign in Russia today against divorce the press and radio will delve unmercifully into the private lives of individuals in order to make public examples of them.

While I was in Moscow the publication *Soviet Sport* printed in embarrassing detail the marital misdeeds of one of Russia's most famous athletes, Konstantin Salnikov, pentathlon star. The article gave the name and described the appearance of his recent mistress, and the mistress before her, to name some of the features. The article concluded, "Just because you are a champion at sport does not mean that you should desert a faithful wife."

Or consider this lead article in *Komsomol Pravda* (the youth newspaper). The headline read: "One's way of life is not a personal matter." The article said: "Vladimir Makarov, a student of the Gorky Medical Institute and Komsomol member, married Ludmila Konstantinov. Ludmila was working and helped her husband materially during the years he studied. This spring Makarov graduated from the Institute. He immediately forgot all the good and kind things that Ludmila had done for him. It seems that he only needed his wife until she had helped him to stand on his own feet. Having obtained his diploma, Makarov, secretly, like a thief, deserted his wife and four-month-old child.

"Vladimir Makarov is working at present in the Smolensk Oblast as a doctor. The Smolensk Oblast Health Department was informed of his disgusting behavior. Comrade Ellengorn, deputy head of the Oblast Health Department, requested the procurator to force the runaway father to help his child and considered that his duties finished with that. Should not Makarov, a man with an evil heart, answer for his own actions to our public? After all, in leaving his family Makarov behaved basely not only to Ludmila. He violated the norms and demands of our Communist ethics.

"Communist morality is radically different from the false, misanthropic ethics of bourgeois society. No general morality exists which is outside class and for all time. The victory of the proletarian revolution marked the triumph of new, Communist ethics. From the point of view of

Communist ethics only those things are moral and ethical which further the annihilation of the old world of exploitation and poverty, only those things which strengthen the new socialist system. The basis for Communist morality, said Lenin, is the struggle for the strengthening and achieving of Communism . . . Socialism has emancipated people, given them unlimited scope for the flourishing of their spiritual life and raised human dignity to a previously inaccessible height."

Before arriving in the Soviet Union I had read, of course, enough to know that the official Communist line on morals had zigged and zagged just as the official Communist line on politics frequently did. I knew that free love and other early Bolshevik tenets were now condemned. But I was ignorant of how far the pendulum had swung. For today in Russia divorce—still possible, but difficult—can ruin the career of a rising young Communist.

Abortion, which was legalized after the Revolution, is now punishable by a jail sentence. And as for the Bolshevik idea that the state would take over the rearing of children, that is emphatically passé. Today all the stress is on the family, and there are some rather remarkable similarities between articles on this subject in Soviet publications and those appearing in American women's magazines. The publication *Soviet Woman* frequently carries long pieces on the role of parental love in giving children a feeling of emotional security and on the dire effect on children of marital breakups.

Parental failure to exercise restraint and guidance is frequently upbraided in the Soviet press as the cause for juvenile delinquency or "hooliganism," as the Soviets call it. Daily the Soviet press carries accounts of teen-age boys and girls being tried and sentenced to prison for crimes ranging from destruction of property (a favorite trick is throwing rocks or bottles at windows of passing automobiles or through store fronts), stealing, drunkenness, and murder. Russia even has its zoot-suiters, youngsters who lean to flared trousers and gaudy ties (the latter providing they have parents who are reasonably well off). But the real target of the Communist newspapers are the boys and girls who go for Western-style hot jazz. Judging from the vigor and continuity of the condemnations, quite a few do.

To promote family feeling the Communists have re-established such things as inheritance rights (a Russian can will his wife or children his bank account and personal possessions such as radios, his car, and his home, if he is lucky enough to own one), life insurance (I was surprised to see posters all over Russia urging heads of households to buy insurance to provide security for their children's future), and a limited amount of private property (since April 1954 the government has provided assistance to those wishing to build their own homes).

In matters of common crimes such as murder, blackmail, and theft there is, of course, an important distinction between ethics for the masses and ethics for the Communist elite. So far as the elite are concerned there are no ethical restraints. The only consideration is whether the means, including murder or blackmail, will achieve Communist ends. But obviously there would be chaos if just anybody resorted to murder. So these crimes are punished in the standard way—jail sentences, Siberia, or the recently reimposed death penalty.

The state is seeking to din not only morals but manners into its people and the press is full of lectures on politeness, refinement, and the sins of being *nye kulturni*. Russia's bosses are quite unabashed at the fact that all these qualities have long been part of bourgeois societies. In Russia these traits are dubbed "socialist politeness," "socialist refinement," or "socialist culture."

There is no denying that the Communist state has done an energetic job of providing the physical props of culture —new theaters, opera houses, museums, and planetariums. In the burst of construction that has marked the last two years new cultural buildings have appeared in virtually all major Russian cities, including such remote places as Barnaul, Siberia, or Tashkent and Samarkand in Soviet Central Asia.

But in questions of taste and refinement the Russian Communist state, like many new civilizations, suffers from a feeling of insecurity and from inability to profit by comparison with more mature cultures outside the Iron Curtain. Many Soviet attempts at cultures seem as heavy-handed and rough-hewn as the peasant stock to which so many Russians, including those in the city, are still so closely related. There is no doubt that many Russian ideas of what is *kulturni* or *nye kulturni* often seem downright weird to a Westerner.

For instance, it is very *nye kulturni* to wear a wrap, even a small jacket, into a Russian restaurant. If you perform this uncivilized act, the waiter will refuse to serve you until you have given him your wrap to be dispatched to the cloakroom. Yet in the same restaurant that is placing such emphasis on being *kulturni,* ninety per cent of the men will be wearing frayed and often soiled shirts, which are usually open at the collar.

My favorite story about Russian standards of cultural behavior concerns an afternoon at the Moscow trotting race track, where every bleacher seat was sold out. I took great interest in watching the Russians placing their bets—you have to pick both first and second place to win—and in seeing horses trotting up and down, apparently warming up. But a half hour went by and the race didn't start. Or so I thought. Although the crowd watched closely, not a sound was uttered as the horses came down the track.

"When will the race begin?" I asked an attendant.

"It's on now," he said.

"But," I protested, "nobody is cheering."

"Of course not," he said, "that would be *nye kulturni.*" He pointed to a notice printed in italics on the bottom of my racing program. At the top of the notice was emblazoned the word "forbidden."

It turned out that instead of being a place to let off steam, a Russian race track was a place where crowds were forbidden to utter a sound. If they did they were subject to immediate expulsion from the track. If their muttering expanded into anything like a roar, they could be arrested.

In Soviet artistic life a fair generalization is that the Russians do best in the fields least influenced by the ideological restraints imposed by the Communist party. Although, as I have mentioned, many foreigners consider that Russia's famous ballet relies too much on scenic displays—fountains, full-scale windmills, and even flooded rivers on the stage—there is no contesting the technical skill of the prima ballerinas of the ballet companies. And some people undoubtedly prefer the Russian super-Radio-City-Music-Hall kind of presentation to the more restrained productions of Western ballet companies. As critics in Western Europe have discovered, Russia has also turned out some wonderfully skilled concert artists, like the violinist Oistrakh. But this is technical skill.

Where ideas are involved—in the theater and movies—the Russians are frequently just plain dull. There have been some relaxations of the ideological reins on writers. Ilya Ehrenberg's new novel, *The Thaw,* while roundly criti-cibed by other Soviet writers, comes closer than other recent works at presenting Communists as they really are. Moreover, under the present regime more humor and satire have been permitted in literature and the theater. But there is still too much insistence that plays, stories, and movies must reflect the stereotypes of life as the Communists think it ought to be instead of the drama and variety of life as it really is. It is difficult to make lively theater out of such subjects as the joys of driving a tractor.

The Russian people find it dull too. This fact is affirmed by the huge crowds that start to queue up whenever there is a prospect of seeing a film made somewhere outside the Iron Curtain. For instance, the Indian film *Brodyaga* (Bandit) was so popular when I was in Moscow that there was a big black market in tickets, which in Russia are bought in advance.

I was surprised to find that the Russians have a three-dimensional or stereoscopic kind of movie which they developed in 1941. I found the small screen hard on the eyesight and the focus bad, although some of the color effects were lovely. The stereo movie I attended was *Aleko,* the Pushkin story of a passionate love affair that went awry.

The only American movies on display in Russia were such ancient but very popular films as Greta Garbo in *Camille* and the Tarzan series. Many Russians tell one with a great air of superiority that the Tarzan pictures are only for children or are *nye kulturni.* But the reason that they speak with such authority is that just about every Russian who has had the opportunity has gone to see the so-called *nye kulturni* Tarzan films.

A telling and amusing summation of Soviet theater was made in Moscow by an American marine guard on duty at the embassy. To relieve the tedium the marine one summer took in some Russian plays and movies.

"I soon gave it up," he reported. "A fellow can take just so much of this business of boy-meets-tractor and girl-meets-quota."

One of the most curious aspects of Soviet culture is the degree to which the Orthodox Church and religion are portrayed in plays, movies, and ballets. For although the government vigorously denounces religion as unscientific, religious life is realistically portrayed in an enormous number of theatrical productions. Most of Russia's great classics of theater and ballet involve church matters. The classics are often performed because so little good creative art was produced in Russia after the Bolshevik Revolution.

It is a strange sensation to pass an afternoon in an atheistic museum and then go to a ballet like *Romeo and Juliet,* where one of the principal characters is a Catholic priest and where the hero and heroine are devoutly religious. One wonders why the government tolerates this religious impregnation of the arts. One wonders how many Russians have kept religion in their hearts, despite the best efforts of the government, simply through constant reminder in drama and ballet how integral to Russian life has been the worship of God.

And it still is. One of the most eloquent reminders came from an archimandrite of the Orthodox Church. Under a system about which I had never before heard, the archimandrite, who is Lebanese by nationality, is in Moscow as a practicing priest (he was the only foreigner to take a degree at the Zagorsk Monastary north of Moscow) and also as a diplomatic representative from the Middle East Orthodox Church.

The archimandrite insisted that the Russians remain among the most deeply religious people in the world because, among other reasons, they are individuals of strong emotion and deep uncertainties, having great need for spiritual reassurance. It was his estimate that even today eight out of ten Russians are baptized at birth.

In his own church, which holds a thousand people, the archimandrite presides over a dozen baptisms a week.

"But aren't most of your churchgoers older people?"

"Ah," said the archimandrite, "you should come sometime just before examinations. Then you will see plenty of young people."

The official Soviet attitude toward the church has changed somewhat since the death of Stalin but the change is only a matter of degree. In the worst phase of Bolshevism churches were physically closed down, priests arrested on a wholesale scale, and parishioners also. I did not see any new churches being built, but the government is permitting the restoration of quite a number, especially if they have historic value. One strongly suspects that this has nothing to do with policy on religion but rather is related to the government's decision to permit tourist trade. The churches, being among the most beautiful buildings in Russia, are natural meccas for foreigners.

Churchgoers no longer have to fear outright arrest. But the government propaganda machine works intensively at spreading atheism and emphatically proclaims that religion and top-flight Communism are incompatible. Much of the Russian propaganda is expressed in Communist gobbledy-gook, odd indeed to anyone schooled in Western theories of values. An example is a recent article on religion in the Soviet youth paper. It began by criticizing a couple who, despite the "honor and trust given them by the award of membership in the Communist party," had permitted their daughter to go to church.

Deploring this departure from the Communist atheistic line, the article recommended the expulsion of the offending couple from the Communist party. The article concluded that in permitting their child to attend church the Communist parents had obviously shown themselves to be a *"pair of hardened idealists."*

## CHAPTER FOURTEEN

## How To Be Happy in Prison

Westerners in the Soviet Union almost always express surprise that the Russian people do not look and sound unhappier. My first conversation with a Russian on this broad question of happiness startled me. It was with my Russian teacher in Moscow, Elena Petrovna, who in her youth had been an actress.

She was describing her holiday in the Caucasus, her family in general, and specifically her amusement in her young son's shy reaction to his first experience of a coeducational school (the law restoring coeducation went into effect in the fall of 1954).

"Life is full of so many things," she said, "I hope I shall live to be a hundred."

"Do you really find life that intriguing?" I said, thinking that there had been many times when I, citizen of a free society, felt rather unenthusiastic about living even to the age of fifty.

"Of course," Elena Petrovna replied. "I want to see if my daughter can become a successful engineer. She wants to be an actress, but I have told her she should find something more secure. I want to help my son become a doctor. I'd like to see my grandchildren grow up. Of course I want to live to be a hundred. Don't you?"

The Russians are not a gay people in the sense of the smiling, bubbling warmth of the Chinese. But the people hurrying into Gum Department Store, or buying ice cream from the pushcart vendor, or even the women sweeping streets do not have the sullen, resentful look of the oppressed. Human beings can adjust even to prison, especially if within that prison they have their families, their friends, and their work.

It would be easy for a stranger who knew nothing of Communist history and methods to be fooled by the atmosphere in Moscow, especially now that Nikita Khrushchev and company are handing out visas at slivovitz (the Yugoslavian national drink) parties and trying to prove to the world that they are jolly fellows and that the Iron Curtain is only a myth created by the imperialist warmongers.

The police state is there all right. But for the most part it impinges only in the negative sense. There are certain symptomatic abnormalities in the average Soviet citizen's behavior. A notable example was the atmosphere in Moscow on the day that former Premier Malenkov was so suddenly demoted from power and replaced by Premier

Bulganin. In Moscow this momentous event, which in any other country would have set the populace agog with excitement, was simply not referred to. There was absolutely no mention of it in the queues before the grocery store, in the subways, on the buses. And a great many competent Russian-speaking observers made a point of checking the public attitude. Outwardly there was no reaction. The Russians did not dare express interest lest it be construed as approval or disapproval and get them into trouble. This is scarcely normal behavior. Yet it is not surprising.

After all, those who would actively resist the Communists are already in jails, slave labor camps, or are dead. The rest of Russia's citizens are those considered by a very watchful regime to be without the will or capacity to oppose them. And as double insurance the state maintains an enormous police force to make sure that no such will or desire develops.

One of the most effective methods of police control is the requirement I have mentioned that every Russian over sixteen years of age carry a passport for use inside the country. No one can move from his home without getting clearance for such a move stamped into the passport by the police in his home locality and from the police in the region in which he intends to settle.

To the stranger the most striking evidence of the police state is the press censorship and the uniformity of information in both press and radio. It is common occurrence for events that are universal knowledge in the outside world not to appear in Russian newspapers until many months after. For instance, Russians asked me why America "is afraid to comment" on a Soviet note charging air violations of its eastern frontier fully a month after the note had been answered and a strong protest lodged about Russian attacks on American planes. The most ridiculous example of how Russians can cross themselves up on supercentralization of news appeared on the day I found two different publications carrying the same economic story. The articles were identical but carried two *different* by-lines.

The only time I saw the Soviet police state at work on a Soviet citizen came in the little town of Gori, deep in the Caucasus Mountains. Fittingly enough this small town is Stalin's birthplace. Gori is situated about sixty kilometers from Tiflis, one of Russia's most picturesque cities, and the capital of Georgia. The Moorish and Spanish accents in its architecture give it a distinctive romantic air, as does its geographical position astride the steep Caucasian hills.

The ugly incident that had its climax in Gori actually began on the streets of Tiflis. As usual the trouble began when I started taking pictures. The crowd that gathered seemed incensed because I was taking pictures of dark-haired Kurdish women, who with their bright yellow and orange costumes had a gypsy look. The Georgians, I discovered, were very snobbish about the Kurdish clans, considering them to be second-class citizens. One of the most aggressive members of the curious crowd was a young student who said he was attending classes at the local language institute.

I had taken the precaution of having the local Intourist representative write a note explaining that I was a bona fide correspondent, entitled to take pictures. I showed this note to my questioners. But the student followed me anyway, and as we were passing through the public park virtually ordered me to halt and give him a chance to put some questions.

"You have no right to ask me to do anything whatso-ever," I said, "but I'll sit on this bench and talk with you for two minutes. Then I'm going to leave because I'm making a trip to Gori."

It soon became laughably clear that he was trying to play the amateur sleuth. His attempts were crude. He made a little speech saying that he was extremely interested in mechanical things, especially tiny watches and tiny cameras. He understood that Americans had great skill in making these gadgets. And if I happened to have any along he would be very interested.

I told him that my only gadget-like possessions were the Russian-made still camera and my German-made movie camera and I proceeded to show him how they operated. After the demonstration, which seemed to satisfy him at least momentarily, I rose and started to say good-by. But he interrupted, saying, "I know the Gori area well. May I accompany you?"

"I couldn't accept the responsibility for that," I answered. "But if the director of Intourist says it's all right, I have no objection."

The young student obtained the director's assent without any evident difficulty. We arrived at Gori just a few seconds before closing time of the Stalin Museum. The town itself with its mountainous surroundings was charming, but there was something grotesque about the ornate way in which the Russians had chosen to immortalize Stalin's birthplace. The tiny peasant hut in which he was born and reared by a proud and respected mother had been kept intact. Around it, however, had been erected a lavish marble building with Grecian pillars. The marble and the carvings seemed to distract from the starkness and inherent dignity of the peasant abode. Although it was twilight, I photographed the scene at some length. Once back on the town's main street, I walked several blocks by myself trying to get some long shots of the little town, framed by the mountain and the sunset. But my film ran out, unfortunately from a photographic point of view, but fortunately from a reportorial point of view. For as I turned back I witnessed something I was certainly not supposed to see.

Two men in dark civilian suits were standing on either side of the student. All three had their backs toward me. The student was gesturing frantically. Then the men grabbed his arms and literally lifted him in the air, propelling him forward, as "bouncers" do when they are throwing a troublesome character out of a room. In the dusk the trio disappeared around the corner.

Until this point I had been astonished into immobility. Recovering my presence of mind, I ran to the car. I found the Intourist driver, a stubborn, sour-faced Georgian, calmly puttering with the baggage compartment.

"What is the matter?" I asked. "Who are those people? Where is Ger [the student]."

"What people?" the driver said, putting down his tools. "I didn't see any people."

"Oh, what nonsense." I snapped, and I hurried to the corner. I could see nothing.

"Perhaps," the driver suggested, "Ger met some friends."

"If those were friends," I retorted, "they were acting in a very peculiar manner."

"It is getting late," the driver said. "We should go back to Tiflis."

This made me angry. "We're going to stay right here until that boy comes back or go and find him. We brought him down here and we can't just go off and leave him."

After half an hour had gone by with no sign of the Russian student, I went in search of the local police head-quarters. They said they knew nothing.

There was another half-hour wait at the car. Then the Russian boy reappeared at the same corner around which he had been propelled so unceremoniously.

"Just where have you been all this time?" I asked.

"Oh," he answered, "I met some old friends and they absolutely insisted that I stay and have supper with them. So you had better return to Tiflis without me."

Despite his attempt to affect a nonchalant tone his voice was unsteady and his hand shook as he tried to light a cigarette. He would not look me in the eye.

"It's out of the question for me to return without you," I said. "Supposing the Intourist director asks about you. Or supposing your family wanted to know where you were."

"If my family should make inquiries, just say that I'm with friends and will come home later tonight by train," he replied.

"But I know you're not with friends," I said. "I saw what happened. I saw the two men pulling at you."

This startled him. After a pause he said, "If you saw what happened, then you will know that it is best for you to do as I say. It will be best for me if you leave now." There was fear in his eyes.

Under the circumstances it seemed that my departure was the only alternative.

Putting the best possible light on it, I could conclude that perhaps the young student's main trouble was that he had been overzealous. Being highly suspicious of me, he had decided in a burst of patriotism to keep tabs on me himself. It is just possible that he was sufficiently naïve to think that my activities were not known—in detail—to the police. If this theory is right, he had mixed in where the police did not want him when he intruded himself as my companion on the trip to Gori. When the police thought my back was turned, they took measures to see that he did not spoil their plans any further.

Later, in a conversation with an Orthodox priest, I mentioned the incident, describing the terror in the young man's eyes.

"Isn't this the kind of thing that builds resentment, creates a spirit of revolt?" I asked.

"Ah, revolt," the priest said, "the outsiders are always talking of revolt. They do not understand the power of the modern police state. Even back in the 1930s when Stalin had had little time to consolidate his power and famine was widespread [because of Stalin's forcible collectivization of the farms] there was no revolt, although never in Russia's history has there been better reason. Today the state has consolidated its position; it has the prestige of having won a great war; it can feed its people; life for everyone is a little better—by our standards. This is not the atmosphere that brings on revolt.

"You Americans do not realize how tired of conflict the Russian people are," he went on. "You must remember that in the last thirty years the Russian body politic has undergone a series of extremely serious major operations, some of them almost fatal. First there was the turmoil and bloodshed of the Revolution. Then there was more bloodletting during the civil war. Next came the second world war. And you may not realize it but this was one war which thousands of us believed our country might not survive. The Germans seemed terribly close to victory.

"Finally there has been the terrible struggle to reconstruct. It still goes on. But at least we are not threatened with more major surgery. Or so it seems. At least there have been no major purges affecting the masses of the population since Stalin's death. Certainly the Russian body politic is on very strict doctor's orders. But so long as we observe the Communist doctor's rules we are at least being allowed to convalesce. This may seem very sad and very negative to you. But most of us, after so much acute suffering, are in no mood to volunteer for another major operation. What we want most is to be let alone."

"But," I protested, "what about the hundreds of thousands who deserted Russia during the second world war? And then there are the thousands who chose exile after the war was over."

"Ah, but they had an alternative," the priest said. "During the war there was help from outside the country. Those who did not want to stay could go with the Germans. That is very different from being all alone when you risk your life to defy a regime."

I found all veteran foreign observers in Moscow unanimous in agreeing that it is difficult to say what the Russians might do if they had a ready alternative to the present setup. Even in the current relaxation of the atmosphere very few Russians are likely to open their hearts to a foreigner to describe what they are prepared to do, if anything, to obtain an alternative way of life. I certainly would distrust anyone who claimed to have this knowledge. It is perfectly possible that in the event of a world conflict many Russians would desert to the West. We know that, cruel as the Germans were, many Russians did prefer them to Stalin. And I am confident that our side would never repeat the stupid brutalities perpetrated by the Nazis. Our psychological warfare experts would indeed be lacking if they neglected every effort to attract potential Russian defectors to our side either in peace or war. But we would also be criminally negligent if we did not prepare for the worst: the eventuality that the Red Army and Russian people are now so disciplined and so battle-tested that they would fight with unprecedented skill and fervor.

In watching the Russians going about their daily tasks, whether in dusty, ancient Samarkand or in Europeanized Leningrad, I was reminded insistently of the lot of the draftee in a giant army. In Russia *everyone* is "drafted." Even the youngest schoolboys are in military uniforms.

Many Russians undoubtedly like neither the sergeant nor the army commander. After all, the choice was not theirs. But every "draftee" knows the terrible retribution if he defies the sergeant.

So, within the framework of the rules, the Russians have learned to make a life. Despairing of change, they try to make the most, personally, out of what confronts them. Most have ambitions of one sort or another: to be a factory director, a sports star, a brigade leader—or even merely to buy a new pair of boots.

Like most foreigners, I was struck by the patient, stoical way the Russian "draftees" have adjusted to the inevitable curse of mass regimentation: endless waiting. There are queues at vegetable stands, milk stores, at doctors' offices, at bus stops.

Even the system of rewards is like an army's: the Order of Lenin, the Order of Stalin, medals for having a large family, medals for consistently exceeding your quota, medals for loyal service to the Communist party.

Communist terminology itself has a military aspect even in the most mundane things. In no other country in the world is the word "struggle" so overworked. It is a "struggle" to cut bureaucratic red tape; it is a "struggle" for culture; it is even a "struggle" for peace.

Whatever their dissatisfactions, most Russians take pride in the material accomplishments of the government. It is the pride of the team member in what the team has done. The Russians take a childlike delight in showing you such things as their subways ("It is much finer than the one in New York, isn't it?" my Intourist guide asked), in pointing out their skyscrapers ("The Americans aren't the only ones who can build tall buildings," my Russian companion said), or in describing the facilities of such landmarks as Moscow's new thirty-two-story university atop Lenin Hills ("In Russia it is not necessary to be rich to go to school," a university professor remarked during my visit).

And certainly any visitor to Russia cannot escape repeated lectures and long statistics concerning the erection of new theaters, palaces of culture, art galleries, museums, and other institutions. The Russians are tired of being called the barbarians of Europe and are out to give the lie to this charge. So deep is the inferiority complex in this matter, however, that it sometimes leads to excessive boasting and thus to an effect opposite to what is desired.

So far as Communist theory is concerned, it is the impression of foreign observers that most Russians merely give whatever lip service is required to stay clear of the political police. And as modern Bolshevik history clearly discloses, the top Communist leadership acts with considerable cynicism, twisting theories to suit its own purposes. No one in modern Russia makes mention of the famous Communist promise of a society where each person will perform in accordance with his ability and be rewarded according to his need. (A highly ridiculous formula, it has always seemed to me, since there is no way to evolve a workable definition of what every individual needs. Who is to say and convince *me* that my needs are truly less than those of my neighbors?)

Russia today is, of course, an example of state capitalism being practiced on a scale unprecedented in world history.

The concentration of power in the hands of a few men is overwhelming.

No wonder Russia's leaders at the top are overworked. They not only decide the general lines of policy but all the details—down to what proportion of steel shall be allocated for hairpins. Every time I went into a Soviet drugstore I used to marvel that the frequent shortages of such things as hairpins did not occur more often. In America thousands of individual businessmen appraise the situation in their own locality and, with their own profit and loss at stake, place the orders that eventually determine national production of such items as hairpins. But in Russia it is some Moscow bureaucrat who tries to decide what that national consumption will be. In Russia it is the handful of men at the top who decide not only hairpins but school curricula, anesthesia during childbirth, literature, atomic energy, TV programs, taxicab prices, and other things. The extraordinary breadth of power of the Russian Presidium is almost impossible for an American to understand because in our own country so many decisions remain matters of private judgment. Imagine President Eisenhower telling a convention of United States architects and home builders that they would have to revamp their styles. Khrushchev did just this at a comparable gathering of Soviet architects.

On the positive side the Red regime does seem to have one important success: most Soviet people have been made to feel that, however lowly their jobs, they are contributing patriotically to the good of the entire country. Time and again Russians would observe to me, "You are working

for your own selfish gain. But we are working for Russia."
They argue that since the Soviet Government is the principal owner and employer all its employees are axiomatically
working for the country as a whole.

I have often explained that in America a successful factory contributes to the over-all prosperity just as a successful enterprise in Russia contributes to general welfare of
that country. And I've said that under comparatively free
economy industries are likely to be more efficient than in
Russia and therefore make a *greater* contribution to the
national wealth. But it is hard to shake Russian belief that
workers in America are exploited, underpaid, and cheated
by private business.

On the few occasions when I have gotten into discussions
concerning respective merits of Russian and American
systems, I have run into an argument that is difficult to
answer—to a Russian. This is the fact that in terms of world
power Russia has come the long way in a short time. You
can point to the cruel sacrifices. You can argue (as many
students of Russia believe) that far more could have been
attained with a freer economy. You can point out that in
fact Russia was on its way to being a modern industrial
society when the Revolution interrupted its development.
But in order to understand the Soviet outlook you also have
to picture to yourself how someone like Khrushchev, the
former Ukrainian plumber, must look back on recent history.

When in Khrushchev's youth the Bolsheviks took over the
country, it had just suffered a humiliating defeat in the
first world war. Then a humiliating peace was signed. The

country barely survived a foreign invasion. Admittedly in this day when questions are being asked in Congress as to whether the Russians are outstripping the United States in air power, it is hard to remember that the world shook with laughter when Stalin proposed the first Five-Year Plan. Impossible, said the newspapers, the statesmen, the economists. It could not be done.

But much of it has been done, even though at a terrible price. Today Russia is the world's second-greatest industrial power; it has the largest army, the second-largest navy (the United States is first, England third), and numerically the largest air force. Russia's rate of progress in production of coal, steel, oil is faster than that of any other country in the world.

There is a big field for speculation in this fascinating problem of how the Russian people have been able, despite their regime, to build tolerable lives for themselves—far more tolerable than most Americans believe possible in the light of the restrictive nature of the government. But I want to make only two more points. First that Russia historically has known very little of freedom. And second that for many human beings a regimented army-like life offers a seductive lack of responsibility. All the big decisions are made by somebody else. You are told what to do, how to act, what to think. The choices are both clear and limited, and you are not faced constantly with the need to make up your mind. If something goes wrong, it's not your fault. It is significant to me that many of the deserters from Red Russia whom I've interviewed complain that once in the United States they have felt a sense of being lost. They did not know how to direct their lives. They wanted someone to give them a definite frame for their activities.

Whatever the reasons, a surprising number of Russians have retained a simplicity and vitality that has permitted them to weather the harsh and oppressive Communist rule without losing the savor of life.

## CHAPTER FIFTEEN

## George Orwell Was Wrong

Despite all the regimentation the Russian people in 1984 will not be faceless robots. The grim society in which, according to George Orwell's book, humankind will be reduced to machines operating automatically at the behest of an all-seeing Big Brother is in fact unlikely to come to pass on this planet, if the Russian experiment is any indication. The Soviet dictatorship has had at its disposal unprecedented technical means for the control of individuals (a life can be ruined in the time it takes to telephone an order from Moscow to Berlin) and a ruthless will. But despite all the Communist claims to the contrary the regime has not altered basic human nature one whit. In fact, from a sociological and psychological point of view, the most fascinating part of Russian life today is the way in which Communism has been forced to accommodate itself to human nature.

A wise old Western European diplomat who had spent in all more than twenty years in Moscow wrote at my request a personal memorandum on the subject. He said, "The Bolsheviks with all their complicated theory, jargon and apparatus came closest to disaster when they tried to ignore an elemental reality. This is that in dealing with human beings, compulsion is never enough if you want a dynamic growing society. Dynamism requires enthusiasm. You cannot *compel* men to be enthusiastic. Or to put it another way, God created most men (let us not talk about the saints and the crusaders) so that they put out the greatest effort when the result is in their interest or in the interest of those close to them. This is not an evil thing. It is natural and healthy so long as any individual's pursuit of his own advancement does not adversely affect the rights of others. Our Western civilizations with their mixed economies (the U.S. for instance has a sector of private ownership; another sector of industries such as banks, airlines, stock exchanges, which are of such importance to the national welfare that they are subject to government regulation; and a third sector of outright government ownership such as the Tennessee Valley Authority) act on the assumption that so long as individual rights are safeguarded, the prosperity of one contributes to the prosperity of all. And actually personal self-interest is indirectly involved even when men give their lives for certain causes. They believe the cause to be in the interest of all mankind and therefore in their own interest.

"But men cannot be compelled to support a cause and

make it a success. There must be a hard core of those who really believe.

"Now in the era of the collectivization of the farms," the memorandum continues, "Stalin tried to rely mainly on compulsion. Oh, there was talk of greater efficiency but nobody was fooled. Everybody understood that the only way Stalin could make the peasantry politically manageable was by putting them in collectives. In resorting to mass compulsion Stalin came to the brink of disaster. He escaped through the ironical fact that under the Czars, Russia was a grain-exporting nation (ten million tons a year) and remained a grain-exporting nation until collectivization. This surplus provided Stalin with an economic cushion. His political heirs are not so lucky. For Russia has never recovered from that agricultural upheaval. But anyway during the collectivization millions of Russians risked death or the concentration camps rather than do Stalin's bidding. There are times when human beings prefer these risks to living on unacceptable terms. And this of course constitutes another reason compulsion has its limits.

"After the near disaster of the collectivization episode even Stalin began to understand the need to harness individual self-interest although it meant such concessions to the bourgeois spirit as giving farmers the right to their own plots of land and the right to a few privately owned cows and pigs. The current regime has gone farther. It has grasped the fact that to encourage personal initiative—and there is no efficiency unless you have people with initiative

—you must allow certain freedom of choice at least in technical matters. Today Russia's leaders are trying on an economic level to delegate responsibility to lower echelons; to decentralize. As you have seen in the agricultural sphere, it is the farmers themselves who must now decide what should be planted in their own localities rather than the bureaucrats in Moscow. Quite apart from the fact that a farmer in, let us say, Tashkent undoubtedly knows more about crops in his part of the country than a Moscow official, this decentralization recognizes that if a person is given the responsibility for a decision he is more likely to try to make a success out of it. He cannot blame failure on bad judgment by someone higher up. Success is directly in his own interest. This also is just another example of how the regime has had to stop flying in face of human nature. The sad thing is that they are not going faster in this direction."

And, indeed, the Communists have reverted to many of the concepts that have traditionally motivated governments seeking stability, order, and progress. They don't admit such reversion. But even though the Reds may call their system of bonus payments to factory workers "socialist incentives," it is, of course, nothing more than recognition of the importance of appealing to individual desire for personal advancement.

Some psychologists insist that the Soviet passion for presenting just about everything in life as the special discovery of Bolshevism is merely a result of insecurity. The Soviet press takes the lead in trying to present age-old human problems as being somehow the speciality of the

Bolshevik age. I remember particularly an article in *Izvestia* entitled, "The Family of the New Soviet Man."

Denouncing the conduct of a certain Soviet wife, the article began: "Major K's wife, the only daughter of well-to-do parents, married during her final year at the institute and immediately gave up her schooling. The husband soon after was assigned to the Far East. At first his wife stoutly refused to go to the Far East and she followed her husband only after strong persuasion and a long correspondence. When she joined him, it became clear that the spoiled young woman was not fit for the kind of life she would have to lead there and that she did not wish to struggle against the difficulties that faced her. She nagged and reproached her husband for taking her 'to such a hole,' complained that her child's nurse was not diligent enough, and demanded that her husband get himself reassigned to Moscow. No, Citizeness K. did not cherish family happiness, did not try to find it. She did not sufficiently comprehend that marriage makes grave demands on both sides; that, as the popular saying goes, to live a life is not just to cross a field [i.e., it's not so simple]."

The remarkable thing about this and articles like it is how very ordinary are the so-called "new problems of Soviet man."

This and other similar journalistic lectures, including those against drunkenness, vandalism, zoot-suitism, murder, and rape, are part of the reaction against the cynicism engendered by Bolshevik mores (any means to an end). The Russian leadership discovered very early that a fixed system of values had to be established for the broad masses in order to curb the widespread crime and moral degeneration with which the regime was plagued in its early days. The government that began by denying that any absolute standards of good and bad existed is now claiming as its own invention such old-fashioned virtues as fidelity, mother love, loyalty to friends, and kindness to the less fortunate. Although these are described as part of "socialist ethics," I don't think very many Russians are fooled as to the exclusiveness of these values.

Marshal MacDuffie, lawyer, writer, and one of the first post-Stalin visitors in U.S.S.R., once observed very accurately that the first big event in the visit of a foreigner usually is the "discovery" that the Russians are people: that fathers take their sons to the park, women flirt with other women's husbands, telephone girls are often snappish, and a sunny spring day improves just about everybody's disposition.

After George Orwell, the Iron Curtain, and the general hostility of East and West, it's understandable that strangers should be surprised that in thirty-five years of Communism so little, humanly, has changed. The surprise works both ways. I am thinking of the Intourist guide who, after a day in my company, observed, "Well, you may be an American, but you don't seem so terrible to me." This pronouncement was made after a period in which the young Russian had watched me with the wary alertness one might reserve for a strange new species from another planet.

Certainly everywhere I went in Russia I found that Soviet citizens possess in varying proportions all the same old human qualities: vanity, selflessness, natural disagreeableness, natural charm, the need to love and be loved, courage, laziness, and so on.

The Communists have not even suppressed such un-natural (in my opinion) qualities as racial prejudice. I was reminded of this during my trip to Barnaul, Siberia. I had just snapped a photograph of a young matron walking down the main street. My companion, a teacher of English at the local high school, said, "Why do you take her picture? She is not a Russian!"

"What do you mean?"

"She is Jewish."

If any proof were needed of how human personality resists stereotype, it was provided by my first encounter with the Intourist staff. The office in question consisted of five girls and a male boss. The girls had all gone to the same kind of school, were approximately the same age (born after the Bolshevik Revolution), had heard the same propaganda, and were city-bred.

But among them were totally diverse individuals. Sonia, as I shall call her, was a tall, strapping girl who would have been a social menace in any society, to put it politely, and not just in her dealings with foreigners. She was widely known around the hotel as the "hang-up" girl because of her habit of banging down the phone as soon as she had finished what she had to say, regardless of the possibility that the other person still had a point to make. Once in my hotel restaurant, to which a hapless Indian had taken her, Sonia upbraided the waiter so loudly I could hear it across the room, sent back her salad to the kitchen three times, and finally stomped out of the room in indignation, leaving the stranger to cope with the bill and the foreign language as best he could. I was told later that this behavior was exceptional even for Sonia. Despite all the excuses it was far from what one would expect from a disciplined servant of the state.

Sonia's opposite was Galya, who had as much natural charm as one could find anywhere in the world. It was combined with a determination to do her best for the person she was assisting. Many of the Intourist girls turned on their smiles according to nationality: with the Chinese, Indians, and Burmese they became graciousness itself because they knew that Soviet Government policy stressed close relations with these countries. Not so Galya. She was the same pleasant person with everyone.

I especially owe Galya a bow of thanks, for it was she who charmed our way into the Dynamo Stadium by talking the director into giving us a special tour. George Orwell's Big Brother wouldn't have approved this violation of state discipline. Technically speaking, the tour should have been arranged through the Soviet Press Department. I'm sure Galya knew this. And I'm equally sure that she took a kind of mischievous delight in cutting corners.

The other three girls in Intourist were of nondescript personality, making little impression, either favorable or unfavorable. The variations within the group of five would certainly not cause any particular comment anywhere else in the world. But they would hardly fit in either with a concept of antlike human beings in an antlike society.

There is no contradiction in saying that the Russians are, on the one hand, regimented and, for lack of an alternative, trying to make the best of the situation and, on the other, basically unchanged as human beings despite Communist pressure propaganda and environmental conditioning. The very fact that the Soviet Union must maintain its mammoth police apparatus to control its citizens is the best possible proof that the latter haven't been molded to Communist desires. According to the Orwellian pattern, most Russians would by now be obedient automatons. After all this time, however, the leadership finds the people so unchanged that it is still necessary to infiltrate police into every phase of national life in order to keep them on the Communist-dictated track.

It is also necessary to use every modern means of communication to lie to the people in order to persuade them to do what the government wants. It would be very simple for the Soviet Government if the Russians were an antlike mass who could be told to build tanks instead of TV sets. But to obtain their co-operation the people have to be given a reason. The government has to concoct an enormous propaganda campaign to convince them that their survival as a nation is threatened by so-called imperialist capitalist United States.

The Communists have not even been able to extinguish the fragile and often elusive concept of freedom. I remember my first interview with a post-World War II deserter from the Soviet Union. He was twenty-one years old and had known nothing else but Bolshevik rule.

"And how do you conceive of freedom?" I asked him, not really expecting much of an answer.

"I know what it is *not*," he said. "In our family we said

with the Czars we had chains of gold and with Stalin we have chains of steel."

In 1984 the Communists may well still have such tight control of the police, of the army, and of modern means of mass repression that they can continue to prevent the exercise of freedom in Russia. But if the lessons of the past are valid, neither in 1984 nor 2084 will they be able to eradicate the desire for freedom any more than they can change the nature of man.

## CHAPTER SIXTEEN

## "How Not To Deal with the Russians"

*One cannot drive straight ahead when one is on a bend*
—old Russian proverb.

Ducuring my stay in Moscow I made a point of
interviewing every diplomat, every businessman, every attaché who had had any experience of negotiating with the
Russians. I did so because, fortunately for me, my trip to
the Soviet Union coincided with my receiving a Guggenheim Fellowship for the study of this subject. In fact, not
knowing that I would have an opportunity for firsthand
research, I had digested something like my thousandth book
on negotiation and related subjects in the period before
my visa unexpectedly came through. So I had a reasonably
good background for my questioning.

This report on Russia as I saw it is obviously not the
place for the detailed analysis and documentation of Soviet

techniques that went into my Guggenheim research. But the conclusions of our negotiators, whether interviewed in Moscow or elsewhere, follow such a remarkably similar pattern that they can easily be compressed into what a prominent American once described as the Points Four on "how not to deal with the Russians."

*Point one: Never expect that personal friendship or unilateral concessions will have any bearing on the outcome.*

As an important American diplomat expressed it, "In the early days of our dealings with the Russians, American negotiators used to give way on this or that point thinking in this way to allay suspicion and create a better atmosphere. This was just giving away something for nothing. It is vitally important to remember that the Russian negotiator is merely a mouthpiece for policies decided in Moscow. He is a messenger boy. Personal friendship with the messenger boy is not going to affect the attitude of the head of the company."

The main difference between the American and Russian negotiators is that the American can make recommendations of his own to his headquarters. His personal estimate of the situation can have a bearing on ultimate policy. The Russian merely states *what has happened,* interpreted, of course, from the good Marxist's viewpoint. This has been true even on the level of Andrei Vishinsky and Andrei Gromyko. Moscow digests their reports, then sends down new instructions. The delay in receiving instructions has frequently proved embarrassing to the Soviet negotiators. During the early debate on the Atomic Energy Commission's first report in the UN, Gromyko was reduced to vague generalities for nearly three months because no word had come from Moscow on what position to take. When Moscow sent the Russian amendments to the report, the Soviet representative seemed clearly relieved that he at last had something concrete to uphold and thence found he upheld his position with great vigor and volubility.

According to available evidence, Joseph Stalin was the only Russian of recent times who could make sudden unilateral changes in policy. And when he occasionally did so at Yalta or Teheran, it was not, in the opinion of those present, out of personal liking for Roosevelt or Churchill but because he scented a bargain. American eyewitnesses think it a great misfortune that Roosevelt was allowed to imagine that he could somehow charm the Russian dictator into good will and that personal regard might be a factor causing Stalin to live up to his agreements.

It seems incredible that any such soft sentiments could be expected from a man who did not hesitate to order the murder of his closest comrades. And the same cold-bloodedness (though to a lesser degree) has been displayed by almost every other member of the present Presidium.

But the American tendency to put things on a personal plane seems deeply ingrained. This was again demonstrated in the recent past when hints began emanating from the White House to the effect that President Eisenhower believed that his wartime friendship with Marshal Zhukov might lead to real progress in ending the cold war. Here again was the implication that intergovernmental affairs could benefit from good personal relations. But in the

Soviet Union there is no such thing as putting international affairs on a personal basis. When Marshal Zhukov writes Eisenhower nicely phrased letters (as he did in 1955 while urging return of a young Soviet escapee), it is certain that this is on instruction from the Soviet Presidium. In fact, some State Department officials thought for a while that Marshal Zhukov was being used by the Kremlin in an effort to get Eisenhower to lower his guard vis-à-vis the Russians. In other words, Zhukov was among the instruments the Kremlin hoped to use in the attempt to obtain the deal most favorable to themselves.

At the Big Four conference at Geneva the Soviet delegation made it plain that Marshal Zhukov had been brought along as a kind of public relations link with President Eisenhower. The fact that the Soviet Marshal was being deliberately used does not rule out the possibility that he has very high personal regard for the President. And it's probably true that this friendship and the wartime experiences in common facilitated exchange of opinion between the two men.

But the exchange of views, which was hailed at Geneva as one of the symbols of the lessening of tension, did not come about *because* of the friendship. Presumably Marshal Zhukov felt just as friendly to the President in 1954 as he did in 1955, even though in 1954 he was still officially called upon to denounce the United States in strong tones. In 1954 Russia's collective leaders had not yet seen the wisdom of invoking the Eisenhower-Zhukov relationship as part of their new tactics in foreign relations. At Geneva, the relationship was brought fully into play after Zhukov was suddenly included in the Soviet delegation even though no comparable official was part of any Western delegation. It was one more proof that Russia came to Geneva determined to turn on the smiles. The personal relationship was invoked because of a Soviet decision at the top taken in advance of the Geneva talks. Not vice versa. It could be called off as suddenly as it was invoked.

The attitude of Russia's top leadership toward General Eisenhower has some extremely interesting ramifications. Some months after Nikita Khrushchev became the apparently dominant power in Russia (although his status remains uncertain) he asked a Western diplomat in Moscow a question that has caused considerable speculation.

"Is President Eisenhower really as naïve as he acts?" Khrushchev asked.

"In what way do you consider that Eisenhower is naïve?" the diplomat parried.

Unfortunately Khrushchev declined to elaborate.

*Point two: In dealing with the Russians don't make "agreements in principle."* Spell out the agreement in detail and include measures for its enforcement. Also include provisions for abrogating the agreement if after a certain period either side fails to live up to its end of the bargain. Avoid any kind of vagueness. Don't use such words as "democratic elections." (The Russians call their one-party system of elections democratic.) Instead outline in detail under what safeguards the elections are to be held.

In discussing the dangers of "agreements in principle" Philip Mosley, director of the Russian Institute of Colum-

bia University, has observed, "The Western powers sometimes gained the 'principle' of their hopes only to find that
'in practice' the Soviet Government continued to pursue its
original aims. At Yalta the Soviet Government agreed after
very lengthy argument and stubborn resistance to partici-
pate in a reconstruction of the Polish Government which
would, it appeared, permit the survival of some political
freedom for the great non-Communist majority of the people. By delays and quibblings over the execution of the
'agreement in principle' during the next few months, the
Soviet Government secured about ninety per cent of the
original position with which it had come to Yalta and thus
strengthened beyond challenge the small Communist mi-
nority in its dominant control of the country. At Yalta the
Soviet Government also agreed, *in return for sweeping
territorial and other concessions,* to deal only with the
Chinese National Government as the representative of
China. By turning over territory, administration, and
Japanese arms to Chinese Communist forces the Russians
nullified in the areas where their forces were dominant
the principal and vital *quid pro quo* which they had promised at Yalta."

The Russians frequently stalled and tried to nullify or
get out of their promises even in smaller regional agreements.

A good case in point, because it is a vivid commentary on
Soviet obstruction at lower levels, is the Hall mission to
Bulgaria of fall 1944. That country had first been liberated
by the Red Army, which had installed a control commission
there. By international agreement at top levels the Russians

had approved American request that the Hall mission go to Sofia with the purpose of apprehending and prosecuting Bulgarian war criminals responsible for the mistreatment of American air crews shot down during hostilities. It was one of the first American missions to begin its dealings in an area newly liberated by Reds at a time when the common victory was clearly in sight.

Chief of the mission was Brigadier General William E. Hall, deputy chief of the Fifteenth Air Force, then based in Italy. The young general was under instructions to do his utmost to get along with the Russians and was personally very anxious to make a success of his mission.

The first setback was, as it turned out, only temporary. It began when General Hall was rebuffed in his efforts to present credentials to General Birusov, the senior Soviet official in Sofia, the capital of Bulgaria. After a long, unfruitful wait at Soviet headquarters the American general and his aides returned to their assigned quarters wondering whether they would even have the opportunity to get started on their mission. But at 1 A.M. a Russian soldier knocked on General Hall's door. General Birusov would be happy to receive him now, the soldier said. When the American expressed some surprise at the hour, he was assured this was normal working time for the Russians.

At their first meeting the Soviet general was the soul of courtesy. Of course he would co-operate fully with the Americans, the Russian promised. There was just one thing of course. He would have to get a clearance from Moscow for the Americans to begin operations. But this, naturally, was just a formality. Considerably cheered, General Hall reported to Washington that the attitude of the Russian general was such that he had reason to hope he could begin his assignment shortly.

From then on the American general visited the Russians daily, eventually three times daily, to ask about the expected clearance. He was treated courteously. But there was no clearance. At first he explained this away to himself and to Washington on grounds of the bureaucratic red tape for which the Russians are famous. It soon became clear, however, that the Russians were just plain stalling. One week went by, then two. On the eighteenth day General Hall went to Birusov's office determined to force the issue.

In their interview General Hall began, "I've been waiting eighteen days for a clearance which I know you could get any time by a call on that telephone [pointing to the one on the Russian's desk]. I can't wait any longer. Clearance or no clearance, I'm going ahead with my operations. You won't like this, of course, and you will get in touch with Moscow. Moscow will get in touch with Washington. Washington will get in touch with my headquarters in Italy and I will be recalled. But when I am recalled I am going to call the biggest possible press conference you can imagine. I'm going to tell the reporters from all over the world that despite prior pledges to my government, despite all the assistance the United States has given the Soviet Union during this war, the Soviet Union made it impossible for me to complete my mission in Bulgaria."

"Why, General Hall," replied Birusov blandly, "I'm sorry you feel that way. For just by coincidence a call came through from Moscow just a few moments ago saying you were free to begin your operations whenever you choose."

The group did eventually accomplish its mission. But if General Hall had not forced the issue it is anybody's guess when—or even whether—the mission would ever have gotten under way.

The Stalin-Harriman (Averell Harriman, then American Ambassador to U.S.S.R.) agreement of 1944 is a spectacular example of the dangers of making anything but a *quid pro quo* deal with the Russians. And, as the head of America's wartime military mission to Russia expressed it, "the *quid* should always run concurrently with the *pro*. Under the agreement in question, Stalin pledged: 1. immediate implementation of Soviet promises for permitting American use of certain air bases in eastern Siberia (the maritime provinces) as part of the joint effort against Japan; 2. transportation priority on the Trans-Siberian equal to the priority given the Red Army; 3. permission for the Americans to send small survey missions to look over the prospective air bases.

The United States pledged: 1. shipment of 1 million tons of supplies to the Far East as a stock pile for Red Army and Red Air Force; 2. delivery to be started at once and to include port and harbor machinery, railroad equipment, and many items which, if the Americans had been suspicious, could have been viewed as intended for the post-war era.

What happened was this. Within a month the Americans had started shipping the stock pile of goods to Siberia. Every single item requested was delivered ahead of time.

In December 1944, after two thirds of the 1 million tons of stock were inside Russia and the rest of the pile, Soviet Chief of Staff Antonov called Major General John R. Deane and said the Russians would be unable to live up to their side of the bargain.

"The requirements of the Red Air Force will not permit granting the use of bases in the maritime provinces to the American Air Force."

There was no apology or further explanation. The Russians had welshed on their end of the bargain and there was nothing we could—or were willing to—do about it.

*Point Three: Don't expect the Russians to behave in accordance with Western ideas of consistency.*

There is a revealing anecdote about Stalin that illustrates this complete Russian obliviousness to consistency in things big and little. It took place at a meeting of the Soviet dictator, British Foreign Ministry Anthony Eden, and Ambassador Harriman. The topic of discussion the previous day had been Soviet intentions in the war against Japan. Eden and Harriman had been so pleased with the remarks Stalin had made on this score that they had decided to put in writing their understanding of the conversation. They didn't want any misunderstanding.

At the next meeting the two Western diplomats handed Stalin copies of the memorandum which had been typed up by their respective secretaries. They asked him to verify the accuracy of their recollections. When he received the documents Stalin flew into a rage. Bellowing at Harriman as if he were one of his own lackeys, the Russian dictator said that in dictating the memorandum the American implied doubt of his word. But more important, Stalin added, was the fact that by committing the conversation to written record security had been jeopardized.

"Stenographers and secretaries," Stalin thundered, "are eager to exaggerate their own importance by telling news to their friends, and thus military secrets are no longer military secrets."

After thus having condemned the written record, Stalin himself produced a *seven-page typewritten document* outlining in detail the goods requested by the Soviet Union for building up stockpiles for the war against Japan. Since it was certainly not Stalin himself who typed the list, he apparently reasoned it was all right to entrust documents to Soviet typists.

The matter of inconsistency continues right on through the present regime. There are many instances to choose from. But one of the most intriguing insights into Soviet psychology was the Soviet complaint just before the "summit meeting" of the big four chiefs of state at Geneva in July of 1955 that somehow the West retained its suspicions of the East. Nikita Khrushchev registered this complaint at a Fourth of July garden party at the American Embassy in Moscow. Yet on the day of the party and the week thereafter the Soviet press, which is of course the Kremlin's mouthpiece, kept up a steady attack against "warmongering United States," its imperialist intentions, and black acts. In Soviet psychology there is evidently nothing inconsistent in expecting someone to trust you even if you call him all sorts of dirty names.

*Point four: Don't appeal to humanitarian motives; instead show how the proposal materially affects Russian power and aims.*

The best case in point was the Soviet attitude during World War II toward American attempts to facilitate the prompt return to the United States of American prisoners of war liberated by the Russians. A brief summary of this negotiation begins in November 1944, when Foreign Minister Molotov, after repeated pressure, finally "agreed in principle" that: 1. there should be prompt and continued exchange of information regarding the location of camps holding American POWs in hostile territory; 2. Soviet and American officers should always be given facilities to go at once to liberated POWs for the purpose of establishing their nationality and facilitating their repatriation.

Finally at Yalta an agreement satisfactory to both sides was signed. It was just another piece of paper. According to the report of America's senior military officer in Russia, the first notice given to the United States of the liberation of its POWs by the Russians was when three of them escaped from a forward Russian camp, made their way back to Moscow, and found the embassy. The men reported that many thousands more, including a number who were seriously ill, were suffering from undernourishment and lack of medical attention. When the frantic Americans took the report to the Russians, it was denied outright. With one exception, the Russians never lived up to their pledge to let Americans make contact with their own nationals liberated by the Russians.

In commenting on the Russian attitude Mr. Mosley, of Columbia's Russian Institute, had this to say: "If the American authorities (negotiating on the POW question) had emphasized that liberated POWs must be well cared for because they were needed in the war against Japan— which was not the case—the Soviet authorities would probably have given much better co-operation in caring for them and transporting them, as they would have been impressed by the direct material interest involved."

In light of the past should we negotiate at all with the Russians? Of course—so long as we understand their tactics. Successful negotiations with the Russians have been achieved—where objectives were limited and aims clearly the same. At the Nürnberg war crime trials of Nazidom's top leaders the Russians agreed to most of the procedures suggested by Western powers and were generally co-operative.

In the beginning of our negotiations with the Communists many of America's difficulties lay in the fact that our negotiators had to deal with the Russians without any real understanding of Communist methods and psychology. Our negotiators tended to judge the Russians in terms of Western values and Western psychology. When serving as a journalist in Berlin I frequently heard Americans complain that they had made this or that concession to their Russian opposite number to show their own sincerity but that the Soviet response had merely been to demand more. And of course Russians are taught to believe that such concessions made by low-level negotiators merely mean that they are not "serious" (a favorite Russian equivalent for bluffing).

In any contest it is vital to know your opponent. And perhaps the most telling summation of the attitude in negotiation of our Communist opponents came from Gromyko during a session of the United Nations. His remark was made in answer to a request by Frederick Osborn, deputy United States representative on the United Nations Atomic Energy Commission. Mr. Osborn said he was sure that Gromyko was sincere in his desire to find a solution for the control of the atom and that he hoped Gromyko believed him (Osborn) also to be sincere. Given this sincerity, Mr. Osborn added, the two of them might be able to get more understanding through a private talk than in public debate.

"Mr. Osborn, you may be sincere," replied Gromyko quietly, refusing the suggestion, *"but governments are never sincere."*

CHAPTER SEVENTEEN

## "Competitive Coexistence"

### Part I: SOME RUSSIAN RIDDLES

It has been said that in modern times the interpretation of internal Soviet politics is something like watching a dogfight under a blanket. You know something is
going on, but you can't tell exactly what.

Since Stalin's death only a corner of the blanket has
been lifted. As of this writing, there are but a very few
top-level developments that could be called even comparative certainties. One is the marked rise in the post-Stalin
period of the influence of the professional military. Under
Stalin the military was frequently purged, as well as afflicted
with interference from political commissars and supervision
by the secret police. There is evidence that secret police
meddling in army affairs has been considerably reduced
since the Russian security police were made responsible to

one top collective leadership as a whole. Under Stalin police powers had rested in the hands of one man—the last police boss being Beria, himself later liquidated—who in turn was responsible solely to Stalin.

The most important single fact in connection with the rise of the military is the appointment of Marshal Zhukov, Soviet World War II hero and a personal acquaintance of President Eisenhower, to the post of Soviet Minister of Defense. It is the first peacetime occasion when a man who is both a national hero—and thus important politically—and a regular army officer has been given one job.

The Soviet military has an enormous potential influence in the internal political picture, especially when leadership remains collective and therefore probably less stable than a one-man dictatorship. The military has undoubtedly been influential in decisions to continue the emphasis on heavy industry, not only because this is essential to Soviet armaments, but also because of Russia's considerable commitments, both industrially and militarily, to Red China. Zhukov and most of Russia's professional military have shown themselves to be highly nationalistic, conservative in world affairs, but as yet lacking in political ambition for themselves.

As to who really rules Russia, the best answer appears to be that collective leadership still prevails, although Khrushchev seems dominant at the moment. I have heard excellent arguments marshaled to support the thesis that Khrushchev is on his way out and equally excellent arguments maintaining that the only place he is going is straight to the top.

Certain it is that this official who holds Stalin's old post as Communist party Secretary possesses energy and cunning. It is equally sure that he does *not* possess the dignity and presence usually associated with a national leader. Although Khrushchev and his colleagues might like to forget it, the world press is unlikely to stop reminding them of such incidents as the slivovitz party with Marshal Tito of Yugoslavia, after which Khrushchev was so tipsy that he had to be assisted to his car.

Little things as well as big point to the continued existence, for the present, of collective leadership. In famous Fourth of July speech delivered by Khrushchev at the American Embassy party in the summer of 1955 Khrushchev warned his listeners not to think that the Russians were anxious to negotiate because they were troubled by internal economic weaknesses. After completing these and other remarks Khrushchev added, "I talked all this over with Marshal Bulganin [Soviet Premier] and we agreed that I should say this. He supports me fully."

Then catching sight of A. Mikoyan, Soviet trade expert, who was standing near by, Khrushchev repeated himself, turning the statement into a question.

"Marshal Bulganin supports me fully, doesn't he?" he said, looking at Mikoyan.

"Yes," said Mikoyan solemnly, "we all support him."

As an eyewitness later remarked, "Imagine Stalin turning to a subordinate to ask for his support!"

Another thing that appears reasonably certain is that the peace offensive is here to stay for some time. Certainly the predictions that the demotion of former Premier Malen-

kov would bring back a tough line internationally have
been proved one hundred per cent wrong. Whatever kind
of a dogfight may be going on internally, Khrushchev and
company seem united in foreign affairs on the theme of
"competitive coexistence."

## Part II: WILL THE "BEST" MAN WIN?

The second big "discovery" made by visitors to Russia
(the first being that Russians are human too) is that the
Russians don't want war. But this is nothing new. Of
course they don't want war in the sense of an all-out
conflict, for this would bring destruction of the mines, the
hydroelectric projects, the canals, the Stalin auto works,
and all the other plants whose construction has brought
Russia into the modern age and which have been the
excuse for all the sacrifices Communism has demanded of
the Russian people.

Russia's rulers are ruthless. But they are also calculating
and shrewd. This is the unanimous view of persons who
have dealt with the men currently at the helm of Soviet
government. And even Stalin, senile as he undoubtedly
was, stopped short—in international affairs—of the para-
noiac tendencies exhibited by Hitler.

Despite their rapid technological advances the Russians
know that any war they started—even if they had the
advantage of complete surprise—would bring the destruction of most of that which Russia's age of steel has achieved.
The situation would change, of course, if Russia became

the first country to achieve a new weapon capable of being almost instantly decisive.

So far as little wars—Koreas, Indo-Chinas, the Tachens —are concerned, Russia can be expected to aid and abet them so long as she feels she can keep them localized or so long as they do not jeopardize some larger purpose, like a really intensive drive for "competitive coexistence." Just what the Russians intend by "competitive coexistence" remains a debatable question. The final answer holds the key to the fate of our world.

According to a Turkish diplomat in Moscow, "Competitive coexistence is Russia's way of buying time to consolidate the gains achieved through the Soviet take-over of some 700 million souls [since World War II]. We Turks have lived next door to the Russians long enough to know how they operate. We know the danger is mortal.

"In five years, or even two," the Turk said, "the Russians will have enough hydrogen bombs to be the kind of threat to the United States that the Soviet Union already is in Europe. Oh, certainly, there may be long periods of tranquility. The Russians have announced that they intend to pass the United States in industrial power. You may smile. But they are capable of doing it. Competitive coexistence is the kind of open sesame the Russians hope to use to get the Western world to help them achieve their economic ends. They want the Western world to be foolish enough to send them machine tools, engineering equipment, and if you will be so kind, some of the transport planes you sent them in World War II or some of the jet engines the

British shipped to them *after* World War II. China needs help too, so she is bound sooner or later to be on the competitive coexistence roster.

"But," the Turk continued, "what if Russia gains industrial power matching—in war potential—that of the United States? When this time comes, you can be sure that the Russians will try to gain their ends first by indirection. They well know how to play on the rest of the world's appreciation of their might—and the rest of the world's horror of the new weapons. It would be typical of the Russians to start with a small nation, like Turkey. Supposing that at the time of Russia's peak military strength she should send a note demanding we turn over the Turkish territory to which the Soviet Union laid claim right after World War II. Or perhaps Russia will demand the Dardanelles. Then what would the United States do? How many in your country would say, 'Should we risk the destruction of Chicago just for a few Turkish provinces?' Or if Russia should once again reverse itself and the target were Yugoslavia, how many would say, 'Should we risk a global war for what is, after all, a Communist country?' This is why we fear coexistence."

But according to a reporter from Tass, the Soviet news agency, "Coexistence is something to which the United States obviously has no alternative. For it is clear that your so-called allies are not going to stand with you in any trouble anywhere. Europe is bourgeois. They do not lightly bypass the chance to make money through trade. (It was Lenin who said, 'The cupidity of the bourgeois world cannot be overestimated.') The more the American capitalists try to restrain the European capitalists from going after profitable trade the more unpopular will America be. Also in Europe they have sense enough to respect the might and prestige of the Soviet Union. A country like France, for instance, is incapable of going to war because, if the French Government declared war, the workers would rise up. The more you Americans express your suspicions about coexistence the more are your countrymen branded as warmongers."

According to an American diplomat in Russia, "Coexistence does not dismay me in the same sense that it does your Turkish acquaintance. It is true that there are some agonizing decisions facing America's leadership. Despite Soviet technological progress we have had and do have (though it may be only for a few more years, maybe even months) such a sizable edge in weapons that we could deliver an ultimatum to Russia in the full knowledge that if the Russians did not respond we could blast their country to ruins. We could say tomorrow, 'Get out of Eastern Europe—or else,' and the Russians would get out —after they'd been told what we could do if they didn't and if they took the ultimatum seriously.

"It's also true that the advantage is slipping from us more rapidly than we realized. Will history say, 'The President of the United States had the power to compel the Russians back to their own borders and thus save Western civilization, but he hesitated and let the moment pass'? Such a verdict is possible. But this is a gamble we Americans evidently have to take. For we don't operate by ultimatum.

"So, indeed, what is the alternative to coexistence?

What is the alternative even if it means sitting by, watching the Russians and the rest of the Soviet world multiply their power?

"But the way to prevent the Communists from using that power in the future, as in the past, will be to demonstrate that any grab, big or little, will bring drastic retaliation. We must be ready to fight for Turkish provinces even at the risk of Chicago. And if we do make plain our determination to fight if need be, I'm sure the Russians would not follow through on their threats."

Khrushchev himself has said that during the period of competitive coexistence the Communists expect "to gain the upper hand" in the world. He gives the impression that this will be done by means short of war (Communism could, for instance, be brought about by revolution from within. And although Communism has never come to power by free vote of the people, this is, of course, a theoretical alternative).

If Khrushchev meant what he said—and it remains in doubt—he is flying in the face of Leninist theory. Lenin's clearest statement on this phase of Communist tactics is this:

"The victorious proletariat in one country . . . after organizing its own socialist production, should stand up . . . against the remaining capitalist world, attracting to itself the oppressed classes of other countries, raising revolts in those countries against the Capitalists and in the event of necessity coming out even with armed force against the exploiting classes and their governments."

However, Stalin himself gave Khrushchev a precedent for

a temporary period of coexistence. And a good reason why Russians may be reverting to this again is that in late twenties and during the thirties the "coexistence" between Stalin's socialism and Western capitalism proved highly profitable—to Stalin. For even though official America scoffed at the Soviet Five-Year Plan, it was American businessmen, engineers, and scientists who did the most of any foreigners to make the plan a success. It would be instructive to know how much of the steel used against us in Korea was made in Russian plants built in part or in entirety by Americans.

Stalin himself contributed some information on the American role in Soviet industrialization when, in 1944, he told Eric Johnston, former chairman of the American Chamber of Commerce, that nearly two thirds of the large industrial enterprises in the Soviet Union had been constructed "with United States material aid or with United States technical assistance."

As far back as 1932 Stalin declared, "We observe the United States with interest since this country ranks high as regards science and technique. We should be glad to have American scientists and technicians as our teachers and in the technical field to be their pupils."

According to a summation made by Ernest J. Simmons in an article on Russia, ". . . American technical aid and industrial equipment played a significant part in the accomplishments of the first two five-year plans despite the fact that at the outset we had not recognized the Soviet regime. To be sure, our own depression at this time stimulated an interest in such a market . . . As a consequence, the annual average of American-Soviet trade grew from under $37,000,000 in 1921-25 to about $95,000,000 annually over the next five years. American Locomotive, General Electric, International Harvester, the Ford Motor Company and many other engineering and industrial concerns not only sold their products to the Soviet Union, but instructed Russians in American plants and in the Soviet Union how to make these and other products. Colonel Hugh L. Cooper and his associates were instrumental in the designing and building of the huge Dnieprostroi Dam, the machinery for which was furnished by American firms. Mr. Peter Bogdanov, head of Amtorg, remarked that in 1930 alone there were six hundred to seven hundred American engineers in the Soviet Union, and he took this occasion to thank publicly the many American companies and experts for their aide in the reconstruction of the economy."

It has been suggested that Russia is reverting to peaceful coexistence because of "economic crises" or other internal difficulties. Secretary of State John Foster Dulles even used the word "collapse" at one point in midsummer of 1955 while analyzing the merits of the capitalistic system as compared with the communist system. Professional observers of the Soviet Union including Mr. Dulles' own brother, Allen Dulles, the head of the Central Intelligence Agency, consider such extreme terminology highly misleading.

A lot of unfortunate confusion about the realities of Russia comes from Western misunderstanding of the Soviet system of self-criticism and the Soviet system of economic targets. As a senior economic attaché in Moscow once explained it, "Russian leaders often announce to the world that they intend to achieve an economic equivalent of, let us say, a million dollars. If they achieve only half a million they indulge in public self-criticism. The outside world, which just looks at the headlines instead of what the half million earnings might mean to the economy, indulges in wishful thinking. Newspapers say that the Russians once again have failed in this or that. The word crisis is used. But there isn't a crisis at all, not in the sense understood in the West. After all, even if you only earn a half million of the announced total you are considerably richer than you were before the plan went into operation."

The most important recent occasion in which the West has invoked the word crisis vis-à-vis the Russians was in application to agricultural problems. It followed Khrushchev's famous January 1955 speech, in which he said there were fewer livestock in Russia today than in 1928 (at the start of the Five-Year Plan). It is perfectly true, but this shortage was also true of 1953, 1952, 1951, and every year on back to 1928.

This doesn't mean all is rosy.

There could indeed be serious problems if the Russians did not take energetic steps to improve their livestock production. The latter has taken on new importance because of the increase in population, the drift of people to the cities, and seven price reductions (since World War II), which have put meat within the price range of more people. All these things are undoubtedly reasons the Russians are giving agriculture more attention than at any time since the collectivization.

There is a perfectly understandable wish in the West to hope that problems posed by Soviet expansionism will be dissolved at no cost to ourselves by Russian troubles at home. But it is also very dangerous to fool oneself about a potential enemy. So if the self-criticism in the Khrushchev speech is to be believed, a look at claimed achievements is also in order.

Khrushchev's January report showed considerable increase in 1954 in deliveries to the Soviet consumer of grains, potatoes, vegetables, meat, butter, and other products. He also stated that the recent past had brought an increase of more than 2 million head of cattle. Additionally, despite droughts in certain areas (notably the Ukraine), Russia in 1954 produced more wheat than any other country in the world, having overtaken the United States both in gross wheat yields and yield per capita. (Despite the so-called crises Russia in 1955 was still exporting wheat to a number of countries, including Iran.)

In his report the Communist party Secretary explained the need for sharp improvement in agriculture by referring repeatedly to the fact that "successive price reductions have caused an enormous rise in consumption, particularly of livestock products."

"Sale of meat to the public," Khrushchev said, "has increased 180 per cent in 1954 as compared to 1940, animal fat 160 per cent, eggs 40 per cent, woolen textiles almost 200 per cent."

Khrushchev has set his agricultural sights very high and even—to go back to the attaché's figure of speech—if he does not make his million dollars he will have achieved considerable improvement if he comes close to his goals. For instance, Khrushchev wants to increase the production of corn to serve as fodder for increased livestock. His plan calls for 70 million acres by 1960! This is nearly 15 million acres more than is usually set aside in the United States for this purpose.

In American thinking the word crisis usually evokes the concept of starvation as occurs sometimes in China or India and as did occur in the Soviet Union during the collectivization of the farms in 1931, 1932, and 1933. But although there are days and sometimes weeks when it is impossible to get this or that product in Soviet stores, there is no hunger. In fact, the average Russian today appears to be better fed than at any time in recent past. Referring again to an observation of the economic attaché, ". . . if there is an agricultural crisis today in Russia, then there has been one every year since 1929, when they started the collectivization. There are shortages, but fewer shortages overall than at any time in my memory. In fact, some of the shortages are political, for Russia plays politics with the ruble. It would be unthinkable for America to export cars if the supply were so short that U.S. citizens had to wait ten months to buy one. But despite the internal shortage the Russians are exporting cars to Belgium, Eastern Europe, and Finland. Anyway, you have to look at things from the Russian basis of comparison. What the Russian remembers is that until recently food was both rationed and high-priced. Now it is unrationed and, even though anticipated price cuts for spring 1955 were not forthcoming, food is cheaper than ever before in recent Bolshevik history."

There is a direct connection, of course, between the drive to increase Russia's agriculture and competitive coexistence. For one thing no nation is in strong position militarily unless it has on hand large reserves of foodstocks. And the build-up of these reserves has been stressed by Khrushchev. If the West does let down its guard during this period and trade increases, the Russians can hope to benefit not only through the import of agricultural machinery but also through the study of Western agricultural methods. A delegation of Russian farm officials in mid-summer 1955 visited the Midwest and reported to the American press that they found new techniques and new types of machinery that could be used with profit by the U.S.S.R.

But will relaxation of tension lead to genuine peace as Americans understand it? The odds remain against it unless the Soviet leaders reach the point where they are ready, inside Russia, to relax their totalitarian system and externally to withdraw from their totalitarian empire, including Eastern Europe.

During this peace offensive the prospect is that official Soviet virulence toward the United States will be softened. But real understanding is ruled out because America is *necessary* to Russia as an enemy. Russia has to have some country to blame for the continuing tight dictatorship and the shortages resulting from its emphasis on heavy industry and armaments.

Genuine peace would also require genuine disarmament. It still looks as if Russia is prepared to do a lot of talking about disarmament but is unprepared to take concrete action, at least to the degree where her armies would cease to be a threat to Europe. Until Russia is ready to give freedom to her European satellites she will need big standing armies to control such countries as Poland, where spirits have not as yet been broken. Also there is something about having massive Russian armies poised on one's borders that makes restless citizens of Czechoslovakia or Bulgaria think long before they plot revolt. And even accepting at face value Russia's announced intention of reducing its forces by 634,000, the Soviet Union alone still has a larger army than the entire NATO alliance, including the United States.

Concerning "relaxation of tension," the most interesting comment came from a British official in Moscow who called this slogan "the Soviet Union's greatest secret weapon."

I retorted that it wasn't very secret.

"Oh yes, it is," he replied, "because the Western world doesn't understand what it really means. The slogan works to the great advantage of the dictatorships and—though we don't realize it—to the great disadvantage of the non-Communist world.

"For the Russians 'relaxation of tension,'" the British official said, "is a handy phrase to bandy about internationally but brings no requirement for any change at home. In a dictatorship you can use force to keep the nation alert and disciplined. Consistency is not required behind an iron curtain. Russia may talk 'relaxation' but at home she maintains national conscription. The Russian aim, it seems to me, is not only to gain time to build its strength but simultaneously to cause the rest of the world to lower its guard.

"Supposing," the British diplomat continued, "Russia were to get out of Germany. By giving up a small piece of real estate the Russians could, I would bet, create an atmosphere where we British would not only be sending her the latest models of our jet planes but supplying spare parts for her hydrogen plants.

"In Britain the mere fact that there was even a prospect of a big four meeting at the summit brought talk of disarmament, and pressure from the public for a cut in the defense budget. The public listens to what nourishes its hopes. Nobody seems to pay any attention to the fact that the Russians talk relaxation of tension abroad but at home they put on a mammoth air show in which they show intercontinental jet bombers which they have been able to mass-produce faster than you Americans."

And, indeed, as the Britisher asked, if the President of the United States cut the defense budget in spring 1953, when the cold war was at its peak and with fighting in Indo-China, what would America do if there were "relaxation of tension?"

As for the Soviet Union, how will it behave when it has a great store of nuclear weapons, the largest standing army in the world, an industrial potential for war equal to that of the United States?

Some optimists hold that the second-generation Bolsheviks like Khrushchev and Bulganin have lost the old revolutionary fervor. According to this theory, the elite of Russia have carved careers for themselves and their children and have a vested interest in the status quo. Therefore they favor permanent peace. It's a comforting theory.

The realities of past performance are not so comforting. It shows that the Soviet Union has attempted to expand its influence with force if necessary wherever the Russians thought they were strong enough to get away with it. They did get away with it in the Finnish war.

In Eastern Europe they are maintaining their hold on a 100 million unwilling subjects who were communized despite Russia's pledged international word that the people there would be free to choose their own governments. In Berlin the Russians were thwarted in their attempts to blockade the western part of the city. But the blockade showed that when the Soviets thought they had the West in a tight corner they would not hesitate to use blunt and brutal force, including the threat of hunger for millions, to achieve their political objectives.

In Korea the Communists came frighteningly close to victory. In North Indo-China, Molotov trucks, Soviet bazookas, anti-aircraft guns, and machine guns turned the tide in Communist favor. And so on.

It is American tradition, as exemplified in the old Westerns, that in a fight the bad man draws first. The good cowboy always wins, of course, because he is the better shot. In the light of past history I see no safety for our way of life unless this country remains the better shot—and sees to it that the Russians know it.

## CHAPTER EIGHTEEN

## In Due Time, or Somewhat Later

There are many things about Russia that make it a natural setting for melodrama. Foremost are the stark contrasts.

In historic Samarkand of Soviet Central Asia, for instance, donkeys remain the principal means of transportation in the streets of the old city. Yet on the golden September day of my visit the main windows of the store fronts were shaken as bright glistening jets swooshed through the sound barrier with sky-shattering noise.

On the road between Kharkov and Moscow I remember parking by a horse-drawn milkcart as I waited in my borrowed Chevrolet at the railway crossing. Yet the train passing by was carrying an impressive number of flatcars laden down with newly produced Diesel tractors—the kind the Russians are exporting to India.

In Moscow the press and radio daily boast that Russia possesses the world's best engineers, best physicists, and best chemists. Yet in all of Moscow there is not a single decent dry-cleaning establishment. Foreigners send their cleaning to Berlin or Helsinki or take out the spots at home.

And in every city of size there is the contrast between the red plush and black bread.

But at the end of my two and a half months in the Soviet Union much of what had seemed melodramatic had become—through familiarity—a matter of routine. And certainly my preliminary apprehensions over my personal safety seemed highly unreal. One of the reasons for all this was that I had arrived at a time of remarkable transition. One of the most conspicuous of the surface changes—and the word "surface" is used advisedly—was in the Soviet Government's attitude toward the foreign press.

When I reached Moscow in early September of 1954, permanent correspondents like Harrison Salisbury of the New York *Times* had warned me solemnly that the secret police had a nasty habit of entering your room during your absence and X-raying film of which they were suspicious, thus destroying the pictures. But by the time I left, it had been many months since the occurrence of any X-ray incidents. The censors were approving virtually every photo submitted by correspondents, and within a few months newspapermen with temporary visas were taking pictures out of the country without even having to show them to the censor.

Also at the time of my arrival the members of the permanent press corps were still virtual prisoners of the Russians because they could not leave the country without an exit visa. There were often deliberate delays of many months before these visas were granted. But during that fall the authorities promised that they would soon inaugurate a system whereby entry and exit visas for the permanent corps would become mere matters of formality. And the promise was kept.

In brief, it was clear that the Soviet Government was soon to permit bigger chinks in the Iron Curtain. Tourist ships were being planned, cultural exchanges were being pushed, more journalists were to be allowed in (although newspapermen arriving in batches in the summer of 1955 were limited to two-week visas). The Russians began adopting the line that the Iron Curtain was a myth invented by Western imperialists. Under these circumstances the element of risk in penetrating behind the Iron Curtain was bound to disappear. On the day I was to leave Russia for home, I certainly did not expect any excitement other than that normally attendant on getting out to Vnukovo Airport very early in the morning to catch my plane. But in retrospect I would say that if it had to occur at all, the melodrama on the evening of my departure was in one way timely: it is useful to be reminded how suddenly the Russians can turn off the smiles and again show the claws.

The day itself had been commonplace. Of the two entries in my diary, the first states: "It is interesting how even the smallest incident can help give insight into such matters as the proletarian worker's attitude toward his job. Today, for instance, at 4:35 P.M. I rang for the valet and asked him to iron a small section of my skirt that had become wrinkled as a result of poor packing.

"When I finally tracked down the valet by going personally to the laundry, he said, 'I'm sorry but I am through with my work.'

" 'But I thought you worked till five? This won't take more than two minutes.'

" 'We work till five,' said the valet, 'but we always start getting ready to go home at four-thirty.' "

No wonder there is no unemployment in Russia. There are more people doing less work at such hotels as the Metropole than I've ever encountered even in the Orient. And I understand that this overstaffing is true of many enterprises, including the collective farms.

On this occasion all worked out all right, thanks again to Father Bissonette. He sent his driver over with his own household electric iron, so I was able to do the ironing myself.

The second diary item concerned a conversation at an embassy reception. It was with a Belgian diplomat who was expounding the theory that one of the motives behind the current Soviet agricultural drive was the government's determination to make lower grades of bread freely available to the public.

"Think of the impact on world opinion if the Russians were able to say that they had the only society where bread was free!" the diplomat said.

It was at the reception that I first heard rumors of the trouble. One of the military attachés was asking me about my detentions by the Soviet police for taking photographs.

"They weren't important," I said, "just time-consuming. I think things are going to continue to get a lot easier."

"I don't know," replied the attaché, dubiously shaking his head. "I can't figure out what the Russians are up to. Did you hear how those Russians manhandled those two embassy girls?"

He was of course referring to the case of Betty Jane Sommerlatte, wife of Karl Sommerlatte, a senior American foreign service officer attached to the embassy. After her illegal detention by the Russians she was falsely accused of the "slap that was heard around the world," as it was later described in a magazine article.

There is no point in going into the details of the case. It resulted in an initial propaganda victory for the Russians, who in the beginning effectively censored the true situation. The result was a great injustice to Mrs. Sommerlatte and the American embassy staff, who under tense and difficult conditions, conducted themselves with remarkable restraint. The full extent of the Soviet propaganda victory was not made clear to me until I reached New York a few days after the story broke. At lunch I was amazed to hear an editor of *Life* magazine remark, "I guess that silly American woman who got herself expelled from Moscow got what she deserved." He could not have been more mistaken.

The essentials are these. Mrs. Sommerlatte and her friend, Betty Stiff, the wife of a military attaché, were walking in the vicinity of the embassy. They stopped and asked a group of women working in a street repair crew if they might take their pictures. (It is embassy policy that all Americans get permission before attempting to take pictures.) The Russian women refused, and Mrs. Sommerlatte did not *even take her camera out of the case* (Russians later issued photos of so-called trash that she was accused of photographing).

At this point two men in plain clothes who had been watching the scene suggested that the two women go to the top of the hill and take pictures of a workers' rest center. The men said pointedly that this would be "constructive" photography as compared with "destructive" photography, and the women accepted the idea. Once they were in the workers' center, it became clear they had entered a trap. They were shown to an airless room and told to wait. This occurred even though they showed their credentials guaranteeing diplomatic immunity. The slapping incident occurred when Mrs. Sommerlatte managed to get to the front door and tried to open it. One of the plain-clothes men deliberately closed it on her fingers, twisting her other arm behind her. Coming to the rescue of her friend, *Mrs. Stiff* slapped the Russian plain-clothes man.

Although the women were finally rescued after being able to get a call through to the embassy, the case caused concern in the foreign colony because it raised crucial questions. Was this a test case in which Russians were serving notice that they would no longer honor traditional diplomatic immunity? Did it mean another reversal of policy, that the cold war was getting colder? The American Ambassador, for one, took a very serious view. He demanded an interview with Soviet Foreign Minister Molotov in order to deliver the strongest possible protest. At this period both the American and Russian press were still

mute on the incident. As is the custom, the American reporters in Moscow had agreed to hold back their stories
until the news broke either in Washington or via the
Russian press.

And since it was the eve of my departure I hoped that
the publicity would be postponed, because if the past was
any example it would involve the usual campaign of vilifica-
tion of Americans. Such a blare of propaganda, particularly
if it augured new restrictions, would have its effect on the
police and border guards, who would inspect my luggage,
which by now was crammed with hundreds of rolls of still
film and fourteen magazines of colored movie film, not to
speak of a half dozen notebooks.

In these times of relentlessly polite Soviet appearances at
international conferences it is hard to recall the other days
of equally relentless hostility. But at the time of my visit the
transition was recent enough so that anxiety could be
quickly rekindled. Like the rest of the correspondents, I
stayed up all night waiting to see what the Russian press
would do. I of course had a special interest, since my immediate future was directly affected. An hour and a half before
plane time the Russians broke their version of the story.

Having confused identities completely, the Russians announced that Mrs. Sommerlatte was to be expelled for
taking pictures of trash (neither woman had taken a single
photo) and abusing Soviet citizens (of which neither was
physically capable, being small in comparison with the two
plain-clothes men, one militiaman, and assorted male on-
lookers in the workers' center with which they were un-
willingly associated during the incident).

The barrage of anti-Sommerlatte propaganda that subsequently appeared—including carricatures in the magazine *Krokodil* of crafty-faced American women taking picture of ash cans—was an instructive lesson in the total cynicism of the Russian press. It can built a case to fit any accusations.

Even by the time I was en route to the plane, the radio was blaring vituperation. Reflecting that there were extremely few American women in Russia who possessed cameras, I thought to myself, "I wonder if I will be mistaken for Mrs. Sommerlatte?"

I had placed all my negatives and prints in a special box so that they could be easily accessible to the customs inspectors. Most of them had been developed and printed so that there would be no possibility of any Russian indirection such as X-raying them. If the Russians were going to confiscate my films, they would have to do so publicly. It was a different story with the color film. There had been no way of having the latter developed inside the country.

At the frontier post at Minsk (White Russia) the two green-uniformed frontier guards who boarded the plane seemed courteous. They told us—there were only two other passengers—that the plane would be on the ground forty minutes and baggage inspection would be done right on board. When I started toward the forward compartment behind the pilot's cabin to point out my luggage, they said they would find it themselves.

"But I would appreciate being present when you go through my things," I said.

"That will not be possible," they answered.

The subsequent forty minutes seemed extremely long. But when they announced the plane would be delayed another hour, the passage of time became unendurably slow.

Finally take-off was announced. As soon as we were airborne I went forward to see what had happened to my things. The Soviet guards had certainly made no secret of their thorough search. My suitcase looked as if a cyclone had passed through it. The contents of my box containing films and negatives had been disarranged. But so far as I could determine everything was intact. I felt I had been very lucky.

I went back to my window seat to watch as our rapid flight took us away from the snow-tinged plains of Russia into Czechoslovakia, our next stop. Inevitably I fell to reflecting about this land which Ambassador Bohlen had described as a country of many secrets but few mysteries.

After two and a half months and nearly fourteen thousand miles I had indeed probed no secrets. But my explorations had at least eliminated many of the mysteries, the seeming contradictions. I had, if not the key, at least a better understanding of the new pattern—a pattern in many ways more challenging than anything we had faced in the age of Stalin. I also knew enough to worry about the lack of comprehension, in my own country and elsewhere, of the meaning of this pattern.

I remembered how at the very beginning of my journey an American businessman in Leningrad had remarked after looking around his hotel room, "Why, we Americans have nothing to worry about. These Russians can't even build a decent bathroom." By now I realized that he had dangerously missed the point. For after one has passed a little time in Russia one begins to understand how the contrasts—the shortage of bathrooms as compared with the progress in building intercontinental jet bombers, the horse-drawn milk carts as compared with the shiny new Diesel engines—are not contradictory but supplementary.

Russia today is a potential threat to the world because Stalin, the absolute dictator, had the power to force the entire nation to "choose" bombs instead of bathrooms. There was not enough natural wealth, productive and engineering talent to go around. Stalin made the choice for all. That is why there have been—and still are—two Russias.

The priority-A Russia is efficient, hard-driving. It is composed of the country's best brains with access to the country's best resources. With the aim of speeding Russian growth as a world power, it is this Russia that is able to produce an intercontinental bomber with less lead time (the elapsed period between the drawing board and actual production) than the United States.

Then there is the priority-B Russia, which as a result of taking second place in acquisition of both material and leaders bumbles along subject to shortages and breakdowns.

Under the collective leadership of Khrushchev, Bulganin, and Zhukov the priorities still stand. The changes they have inaugurated in the pattern of modern Russia are of degree, of manner. Smiles have been, when convenient, substituted for frowns because the new leaders had sense enough to realize that the ruthless extremes of the senile Stalin's last days were working to their disadvantage.

Most of the changes have cost Russia absolutely nothing and gained her much. The disappearance of such cruel laws as those forbidding Russian wives of foreigners to leave the country is an example. Russia's agreement to the reunification of Austria would on the surface seem an outstanding exception. It remains to be seen whether Soviet implementation of an accord to which they agreed "in principle" many years ago will prove a net gain or loss. If the example of a neutralized Austria can act as a magnet for divided Germany and the rest of Europe, it will be an overwhelming gain.

For anyone who has visited Russia—in fact, for anyone who has seen the pendulum of opinion swing from adulation to hysterical fear—the most important guide is to keep an eye on what is done in Russia, not what is said.

Russia went to the Big Four "summit conference" at Geneva, for instance, determined to apply her new philosophy of international public relations. This made the atmosphere far more pleasant. But this did not prevent the Russians from rejecting all key Western proposals, including those for a reunited Germany free to decide its own future. Nor did all the conversations between President Eisenhower and his wartime friend Marshal Georgi Zhukov about their mutually peaceful aims hide the fact that the Soviet defense budget for 1955 is twelve billion rubles more than 1954; that Russia has put more intercontinental jet bombers into the air than the United States; that

Russian potential for war—coal, steel, and iron—is increasing at a faster rate than that of any other country, including the United States; that Russia has more submarines than did Nazi Germany at the outbreak of World War II.

It is an understandable but unfortunate tendency of a peace-hungry world to mistake signs for reality. It is also a tendency to disregard what the Russians say if it is not pleasant. Communists are not subtle; people like Secretary Khrushchev or Premier Bulganin do not hesitate to say that "Communism will gain the upper hand" in the world or that "nothing can stop the march of world Communism." It is a lucky advantage for them that so many Westerners choose to believe that these men can't really mean what they say. The Russians have all the psychological head start of the *enfant terrible* who shows signs of reforming. If Premier Bulganin goes to an international conference and acts courteously, it makes world headlines: "Russian Affability Eases International Tension." If British Prime Minister Anthony Eden goes to an international conference and acts courteously, it is taken as a matter of course. It is remarkable that the Russians repeatedly pull off the trick of getting credit for doing things that are considered natural in any other civilized country.

With results to which I have been personal witness in Geneva and elsewhere, Russian affability has already done much to persuade the West to lower its guard. A few conciliatory gestures here and there may well enable Russia's leadership to gain more at less cost than was ever possible under Stalin.

The Stalin period saw the coining of one famous slogan:

"In the second half of the twentieth century all roads lead to Communism." But under Stalin the road was bumpy, dangerous, often treacherous.

Russia's present leadership is changing the Communist road this much: they are widening and smoothing this highway to Communism so that their prospective traffic can get to its Communist destination all the more quickly. It is up to the Western world to keep its sense of direction, post the right highway markings, and see to it that the travelers are clearly warned they are heading for a dead end.

Once at the beginning of the cold war I asked Marshal Vassily Sokolovsky, then military governor of East Germany, if there would ever be any real changes in the Soviet system. He did not reply directly but instead asked me to repeat after him a Russian phrase: *"Svoye vremina, ili nye skolko poshe."* His English-speaking aid translated it to mean: "In due time, or somewhat later."

It's still as good an answer as any.

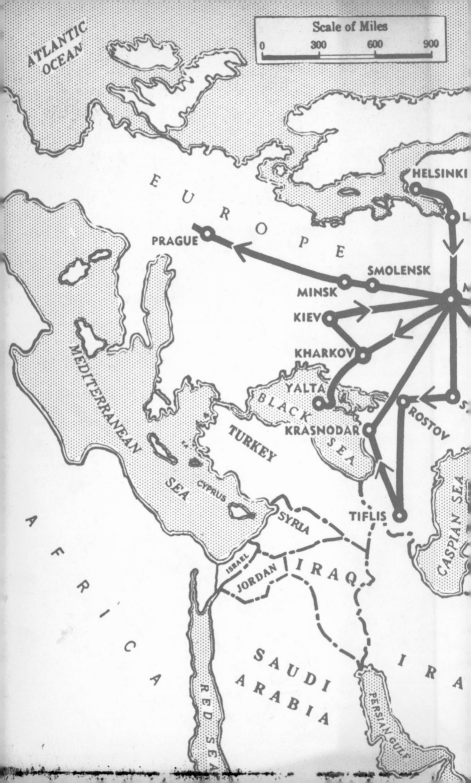